LEADING LOCAL TELEVISION

HANK PRICE

ISBN 13: 2018958677
Library of Congress Catalog Number: 978-1-64343-979-2

22 21 20 19 18   5 4 3 2 1

Edited by Sara & Chris Ensey
Cover and interior design by Laura Drew

Beaver's Pond Press, Inc.
7108 Ohms Lane
Edina, MN 55439–2129
(952) 829-8818
www.BeaversPondPress.com

For Maria, Pepper, Harper, and Courtney—
MORE IMPORTANT TO ME THAN ANY TELEVISION STATION

Contents

PREFACE

It's hard to believe that, two decades into the twenty-first century, local television is still a viable business, much less our nation's single most important form of communication. We live in a world of fragmented media and constant change, so it's easy to forget that local television is not just viable; it is the last form of mass communication.

A logical reading of history would say local newspapers, with their massive databases and community connections, should have used new technology to morph into dominant local brands. Newspapers missed their opportunity, leaving the field clear for television. Will television make the same mistake of being so bound by culture it cannot see the future? Many stations will. But for a few, the future will bring dominance in local information unlike anything imaginable in the past.

The key to that future, to local dominance, is brand. The key to brand is effective leadership. A second key is ownership. Only owners committed to the future can create the future. But no owner, no matter how committed, can create the future without effective local leadership.

I've spent a good part of my career, both in the commercial and educational worlds, trying to help talented department heads become great general managers. Therefore, this book is also written for those who aspire to be local leaders, the kind of change agents who will take the idea of brand dominance to far greater heights and success than my generation ever contemplated.

1

But I Thought Television Was Dead

In the fall of 1970, I was a young kid in my first job at WJTV, the CBS affiliate in Jackson, Mississippi. One afternoon that fall, our entire staff was told to assemble in the main studio for a mandatory meeting called by Owens Alexander, WJTV's station manager. Mr. A was not in a good mood:

"For the past twenty years, television has been a great business we've all benefited from, but those days are about to end. The best days of television are behind us.

The largest and most important advertisers we have, both on our station and the networks, are cigarette companies. Cigarettes pay your salaries and mine, pay the light bill, pay to support network news, pay to create network programming. At least, they did. Congress and the tobacco companies have reached an agreement that, beginning in January of 1971, cigarettes will no longer be advertised on television. Television as we know it is over. Prepare to tighten your belts. I'm sorry to tell you this, but you have a right to know."

Pretty stunning news to a twenty-one-year-old looking forward to the future. As it turned out, the loss of cigarette advertising did hurt television for a while, but other advertising categories grew until, gradually, the "cigarette crisis" was forgotten. The best days turned out to be ahead, not behind.

Ten years or so later, during the 1980s, the growth of cable sent shock waves through the television industry. New cable networks seemed to be launching every day. Consumers eagerly signed up to have their homes wired. The mood at television stations was one of crisis. Cable was going to take our audience and our advertising. National articles in our own trade magazines proclaimed cable would soon overwhelm traditional broadcasting. There was much speculation that CBS, NBC, and ABC would soon be able to bypass stations and go directly to consumers via cable. William S. Paley, the famed founder of CBS, even proposed starting a national cable news channel. When his board expressed fear of an affiliate revolt, Paley backed off, but an Atlanta entrepreneur named Ted Turner grabbed the idea and launched his own news network, giving it the not-exactly-creative name of Cable News Network.

The cable crisis caused a number of my friends to get out while they could. They were convinced local television was about to die.

Of course, cable did not destroy local television, nor did the networks bypass their local affiliates. Cable did fractionalize audience and revenue, but station profits still continued to grow.

The next crisis came in the early 1990s. Deregulation had more than doubled the number of television stations in the United States. Many of those stations were adding local news. There was even talk of a fourth network. Common wisdom was that dividing the advertising pie so many ways would destroy profits. The cost of programming would also skyrocket.

As it turned out, the number of stations did double, the formation of Fox fractionalized audiences, and the cost of quality programming did go up, yet the advertising pie still grew. So did profits.

It's interesting to note that back in those days, the average television station produced less than three hours of local news a day. Today, it is not unusual for an affiliate to produce three hours of morning news alone.

The explosive growth of the internet in the early 2000s brought on the next crisis for local television. High-speed internet connections were spreading from offices to homes, giving consumers fast access to a world of new information and entertainment. The introduction of the iPhone in 2007 took the internet mobile. Predictions of a massive movement of audiences to the internet, plus the body-blow recession that began in 2008, caused analysts to wonder if television could possibly continue as a viable business. At the very least, the herd would be thinned, leaving far fewer stations producing local news.

As it turned out, both viewers and significant advertising dollars did go to the internet, and that did compress television profits. Television's greatest weakness had always been its dependence on advertising alone as a single revenue stream. That meant the loss of advertising dollars was a potential killer.

But then an amazing thing happened. During the mid-1990s, stations had gained the legal right to charge cable and satellite services to carry their channels. Faced with universal refusal by systems to pay, most station owners backed off, but one then-small owner refused to give in. Nexstar television was the first group broadcaster to take stations off cable for refusal to pay. After months of pain for both Nexstar and the cable companies, the companies finally agreed to pay compensation. With the dike breached, other broadcasters quickly followed suit. Spurred on by a recession hitting television profits, companies realized how underpaid they were by cable systems compared to cable-only networks. Faced with no other good choice, broadcasters began to play hardball with cable and satellite providers.

The addition of retransmission consent revenues from cable and satellite companies saved the status quo of local television.

Retransmission dollars, supplemented by web and secondary channel advertising revenue, finally made television a true multi–revenue stream business. Because a portion of retransmission revenue was shared with the networks, they also grew stronger, funding network programming and, most importantly, ensuring the station-network relationship would survive.

Over the past fifty years, television overcame each of these threats, and others along the way, because television always morphed, finding new revenue streams and new efficiencies. Profit margins became smaller but still were massive when compared to other industries.

I'd like to say those of us in local television have been smart enough to see the future coming and plan for it, but that has never been the case. Each time television morphed into something new, it was because the industry was faced with no other choice. Still, that is not to take away from the fact the industry did morph, survive, and profit through each crisis.

Why did this happen? What's the secret sauce? Why does a 1940s technology continue to dominate local news and information moving into the mid-twenty-first century? The answer is it is not about technology at all. Technology has simply been an enabler. The secret sauce is the relationship leading television stations have with the local viewers they serve. That is the reason local television stations are still relevant.

But what of the future? The evidence suggests local television will not only survive but also thrive. Not all stations and not necessarily in their current forms, but thrive they will, in part because the only other major providers of local news and information—newspapers—have taken themselves out of the game.

The most likely scenario is that stronger local stations will become launchpads for brand-based local information businesses. ATSC 3.0, combined with 5G, is a perfect platform for brand extension. As technology continues to expand, so will other new opportunities. Traditional television will still matter, but it will be part of something much bigger, far more complex, and probably even more profitable.

If you take nothing else from this book, please understand that a successful future will not be about technology, fixed business models, or many of the things that got us this far. In fact, the culture that we have so carefully built over the past seventy years is in some ways now our greatest obstacle. All those things are important tools, but they are not the core of a station's value. The future is about growing our relationship with local consumers. That means the future is about brand value.

Local television station brands have value because they are important to local consumers. A brand is about a relationship. Consumers choose to give the relationship value because they trust a station's brand.

With the demise of local print and the incredible fragmentation of other media, local television is the only total-market brand left standing. That means there is room for the relationship to grow in new ways, many of which don't yet exist. Not every station will survive, but those that do have bright futures. The key is to use their powerful current platforms as launchpads to the future.

How difficult will achieving that future be? Nurturing and growing a brand is complex and fraught with danger. One major failure of trust, and consumers are gone. Yet done right, I am convinced the future can be more exciting, more fun, and more profitable than anything in the past.

If brand is the key to the future, what is the key to brand? That is what this book is about. The key is leadership. The key is you.

2

Why Leaders Have Power

Leadership's Bottom Line

There is an old broadcasting truism that says, "Walk into any television station and you will immediately know if that station is in first place or last just by the feeling of energy in the building." While a little exaggerated, I've found the statement in principle to be true.

Television is a team sport that runs on energy, pride, and emotion. Great television stations reflect those characteristics in the attitudes and energies of their staffs. From the switchboard operator to the production assistant, everyone knows they are part of the leading, or soon-to-be-leading, station. When that sense of pride, mission, and joint effort is missing, usually the ratings are too.

Great television stations are complex organizations, but their root dynamic, the one driving force they all share, is a sense of mission: a clear understanding of their goals and reason for being. That doesn't just happen. It's the result of ongoing, effective leadership.

The reverse is also true. Stations on the decline, or those that have never experienced the excitement of winning, usually share a sense of lethargy undergirded by fear of the future. There is widespread belief that the status quo is permanent, that nothing will ever get better. Stay in the building long enough and you will begin to hear the excuses. Stories of past failures, unsupportive management, underfunding, the wrong network, the wrong owner, whatever justification seems to fit. All are ways of saying, "I know things will never get better. Don't blame me. It's not my fault." These attitudes are also the result of leadership.

Leadership starts at the top and always comes down to one key player: the general manager. Like it or not, a station usually reflects the leadership ability of its GM. The success or failure of an organization is, of course, more complex than just the leader, but I've found that truly great stations virtually always have great leaders. It also works the other way. More than one strong station has been decimated by poor leadership.

Both success and failure are rooted in leadership. There is no way to escape this reality.

Why Leadership Always Matters

In order to be a successful leader, one must first understand why leadership has such a profound effect on any organization.

It is only natural that people in any business look to the person in charge for guidance. Most employees have an inherent understanding that their own careers are directly tied to their leader. It's a pretty simple proposition. Competent, secure leaders create a sense of security, strength, and positive perspective for employees. Insecure or incompetent general managers radiate failure.

Like it or not, employees put managers in a bubble, observing their every action and mannerism. Something as simple as a manager not acknowledging an employee while passing in the hall can be seen by the employee as a devastating criticism. Unfair to the manager? Of course it is. But that's the way human nature works. The good news is that general managers who are aware of their power can use it to constantly build an organization up.

Great general managers come in many types, ages, races, and sexes, but they all share the unique ability to project a vision and help others take that vision as their own. The list of things that can destroy a television station is a long one. Lack of resources, unfortunate decisions during times of crisis, failure to build an effective organization, and even poor ownership can derail a station. But building a great station, or even maintaining one, cannot be achieved without an effective leader projecting a clear vision that employees understand and buy into. No amount of resources, organizational ability, or corporate backing can make up for visionless leadership.

Leadership is not about a particular style, nor is it about fitting into some kind of universal mold. What great leaders share is a firm belief in what they are doing, a determination for the organization to succeed, and the ability to empathize with staff. Always competitive by nature, the best see the world in terms of winning and losing. Whatever their vision, it inherently involves some form of "winning." In the past, defining winning in television was easy: have the best news ratings, highest sales, and largest profit. In today's multiplatform, brand-centric world, nothing about winning is easy. Those who live in the past will be overwhelmed. Yet for those willing to do the heavy lifting required to build a modern media entity, the complexity and rewards of winning can be more satisfying and more fun than anything in the past.

It may be obvious, but still worth saying, that the bottom-line measurement of "winning" is always profit. Not profit for a quarter or a year, but sustainable long-term profit.

We live in a society in which some see profit as a bad word. It is not. No organization can provide good, high-paying jobs without reasonable profit. Profit brings long-term stability to a station, giving employees the opportunity to build careers, support families, and be productive members of their communities. Never apologize for making a profit. To not do so is to go out of business.

Great leaders also understand that how one wins also matters. A person who wants to win at all costs courts disaster. To achieve greatness, a leader must see the bigger picture, understanding that success only matters if it can be sustained. That means balancing short- and long-term decisions.

Great leaders also possess an essential understanding of their own motivations. Personal insight is essential because it helps give perspective. Perspective is a building block that guides one's understanding of which paths lead to success and which to dead ends or worse. Perspective also lessens the fear of failure. Great leaders have already thought about the consequences of failure and realized they can live with them. What they cannot live with is knowing they never tried. Realizing that failure is not the end of the world allows a leader to learn from mistakes, accept the consequences, then move forward without the destructiveness of embedded fear. A reasonable level of fear is healthy, even needed, because it makes a person consider all options. But fear must be kept in check as a lane marker, not a stop sign.

As we think about the foundational role television will play in the future of local media, it follows that innovating the future must be built on current strengths. Innovation by weaker players is rarely successful because they lack existing user support. In other words, if you want to create the future, you must begin by doing the hard work of creating a powerful existing organization. That job requires leadership.

Start with Your Own Motivation

Before you can take on the task of creating an organizational vision, you must first understand your own motivation. What are your personal career goals? Why are you doing this job? Are you looking for acclaim, promotion, money, the thrill of winning? Self-examination is important because your career goals will drive not only your leadership style but every other aspect of how you view the organization. What are you willing to do to succeed? What are you unwilling to do? It would be nice to say that motivation is always altruistic, but human nature does not work that way. Honesty about your own self-interest is the first step in understanding how to motivate others to fulfill their own self-interests.

It has been my experience that general managers who derail often do so because they have no clear personal goals for the future. This lack of expectation causes them to become vulnerable to shifting personal priorities and changing expectations. They inevitably end up in defensive mode, seeking to protect rather than advance. Employees see this and immediately follow suit, making defensive decisions of their own. This virtually always results in decline.

Some new general managers suffer from what I call "the arrival syndrome," always a career killer. This happens when a person feels he or she has worked his or her entire career to achieve this position and now expects subordinates to treat him or her with deference.

Equally unfortunate are general managers who are not prepared to take on the harder parts of the job, such as holding people accountable, being truthful in difficult situations, and trusting department heads to do their jobs. The result is inconsistent decision-making. Employees always recognize inconsistency. This makes them fearful because they do not know if they will be rewarded or criticized for any particular action.

Leaders who take the time to analyze their personal goals inevitably come to the conclusion that the best way to reach those goals is to have the organization they lead excel. For that to happen, members of the staff must also excel. There is no escaping this simple fact. If you want to achieve your personal goals, the best way to do that is by helping others achieve theirs.

Consider this. Every time someone who reports to you achieves greatness, that greatness is also a part of your success. I have personally found my greatest satisfaction comes when people who once reported to me become successful general managers themselves.

Of course, different people have different motivations. Whatever your motivation, it must result in a desire to achieve long-term success for both ownership and employees. If that is not your goal, get out now because misery and failure are in your path.

The Power of Authenticity

Some people are naturally blessed with what we usually think of as leadership skills: an outgoing personality, visible drive, and likability. If you have these things naturally, then great. Those things are helpful, but they are not essential.

This is not to say social skills are not required. A person so introverted that he or she doesn't enjoy being with people is probably not going to become a great leader.

Real leadership is not about personality. I've known dozens of people with great personalities who were not great leaders. Learning to be an effective leader is hard work. It means building skill sets that are not always natural and doing so over a long period of time. One of those skills is choosing to criticize yourself. There are a number of ways to do that, including formal tools such as 360-degree feedback, but simply listening to other people while keeping an open mind may be the most effective.

I remember getting back one particular 360-degree survey early in my management career. It said department heads were frustrated because when they sat down to talk with me, I never gave them my full attention. That was a revelation. I thought I was good at multitasking. Instead, I was being offensive. Starting that day, when someone came into my office, I put aside whatever I was working on and gave him or her my full attention. I also learned to say things like, "Have a seat and give me just a moment. I want to finish this so I can give you my full attention." It was one of the best lessons I ever learned.

No manager is going to be perfect, but continuing self-evaluation is a powerful tool that can help you become a more authentic leader. If you believe you don't need self-evaluation, then you are going to make mistakes that could easily be avoided.

I once knew a management consultant named Dr. Bob Terry who wrote a number of books on authenticity. Terry's main point was that in day-to-day relationships, people always know if you are being straightforward with them. Inauthenticity on a leader's part causes staff to lose confidence and wonder what else the leader is not sharing. The resulting whispers and "real agenda" conversations can destroy an organization's ability to grow and move forward.

Take, for example, the manager who always says "everything is going well" when in fact everyone knows things are not well. If goals are not being met, things are not going well. It is far better to face these things head on, acknowledging failure and verbalizing the truth. Every organization faces challenges and sometimes misses expectations. Well-led organizations are able to put misses and failures into the context of a bigger picture. What did we learn from this? How do we plan to go forward? What path must we now take to achieve our long-term goals?

Winning by Putting Yourself Last

Part of authenticity is sometimes subverting your own wants and needs for the greater good of the organization. For example, there is nothing wrong with having a reserved parking spot, but there is a lot wrong with traveling first class on the same plane as subordinates who are in coach. People expect the leader to have reasonable perks, but when employees see their boss taking advantage for personal gain, motivation drops like a rock.

Years ago in Minneapolis, our neighbor John Dasburg was running Northwest Airlines, a company he had been brought in to save. After successfully renegotiating contracts with a half dozen employee unions, John was embarrassed when the local paper announced the Northwest board had given him a $500,000 bonus. You can imagine how the employees felt. John immediately, and publicly, rejected the bonus. He also rejected increased stock options and any other long-term compensation that would make up for the loss. It must have been a hard thing to do, but it saved John's relationship with Northwest's rank and file. It may have saved the company.

Recently, an employee said to me, "You can do anything you want because you're the boss." My answer was, "Actually, I'm the last person able to do anything he wants." Whatever the leader does, others will follow.

Consider this. If the organization you lead excels, you get the credit. If the organization fails, you cannot escape blame. Keeping your eye on the bigger prize, the long-range career and financial rewards that come from running a successful media company, allows you to forgo small rewards that are usually not worth the walls they raise between you and your staff.

Why the Emperor Has No Clothes

Anyone who has been in top management will tell you that the higher you go, the more isolated you become. This happens not because of anything you have done but because of the expectations of your staff.

As much as you would like for people to see you as yourself, it is unfortunately not possible for them to completely separate the position from the person. Every interaction with you is seen through the lens of your position in the company. That means every interaction is driven in part by how that interaction might affect their job, their income, their future.

I often tell new general managers that most people who come into their office are, on some level, intimidated. The pressure to only give good news is intense. The pressure to avoid blame for bad news is equally intense. The higher your position, the more intense the pressure on those reporting to you. This is why the emperor has no clothes. People who never think of themselves as "sucking up" actually do it all the time. Often, they don't even realize what they are doing. And these are the normal people, not those intentionally trying to gain favor.

The problem is most acute with people you don't personally supervise. Many members of your staff, especially those separated by several management levels, will simply avoid coming to your office, thinking instinctively that there is little to be gained and much to be lost.

One day shortly after I got my first GM job, I happened to park my car at the same time one of our account executives did. As we both got out of our cars, I jokingly remarked that she was calling on clients in an awfully run-down car. I later found out she went directly to the general sales manager's office and broke down in tears. After composing herself, she drove to a dealer and traded in her car. All that from a thoughtless joke.

Speaking of account executives, throughout my career, I've asked the AEs to take me out on sales calls. Few have accepted the offer. I've resorted to having the local sales managers make it a requirement. Why would they not want the GM on calls? It's because most AEs do not want the GM to be looking over their shoulder, judging how well they perform with a client. That is not my purpose, but my purpose does not matter.

As a senior leader, you are, of course, tempted to accept your position and enjoy the praise, fear, power, and other ego-building perks of being a general manager. This is a terrible mistake that can cripple an organization. If you are going to make great decisions, you need accurate information and honest ideas, not people telling you how right you are. Thus, you need ways to build bridges to your staff.

Turning Barriers into Advantages

Your greatest asset in building bridges is your own attitude. You have a big ego—otherwise, you would not have risen this far—but you also know deep down that you are not always right. You must constantly remind yourself that you do not have all the answers. You need both good information and great ideas. The most accurate information and best ideas often come from the rank and file: master control operators, photographers, engineers—the people who touch the product and live in the community. They can be some of your best sources. You will only learn this information if you are able to get them to speak to you the same way they speak to each other.

Time after time in thirty years of managing stations, I've learned facts from regular employees that department heads would rather not share, have slightly shaded, or may not even be aware of. These have come from normal conversations, based not on my role as the GM but as someone who knows their names and something about their families and is willing to have a non-threatening passing discourse.

Of course, not all ideas that come from employees are good ones. The temptation is to brush those off, but you will be better served by taking a few moments for a serious discussion. Explain why the idea won't work while also praising the employee for creative thinking. If possible, find some part of the idea you really like or at least are willing to consider. You don't have to accept the idea. You just have to show respect.

Not too long ago, I learned that the wife of a longtime AE had been diagnosed with cancer. I made a point of asking how her treatment was going on a regular basis. During the following months, the AE's productivity dropped because of the time he had to spend on his wife's treatment. Both his manager and I assured him we understood and knew his productivity would return to normal once the crisis was over.

Once the AE's wife was on the mend, I stopped asking about her. One day in the coffee room, the AE said, "My wife asked this morning if I had seen you lately and given you an update." What was just part of my job turned out to be very important to someone who wanted continuing reassurance during a family crisis.

Your first and most important tool in building bridges is simply walking around. The more employees see you, the more comfortable they become. Calling people by name, asking about their families, and broaching subjects completely unrelated to work are powerful tools. The more staff members are used to seeing you, the more they open up. The key is brief, nonthreatening conversations on a regular basis.

Caution—remember that these conversations must be authentic. Your goal is to break down barriers, not create false camaraderie. If you are not genuinely interested in a person, he or she will know it immediately. He or she will also know when you are genuine. How do you be genuine? Make a conscious decision to actually care about your staff.

Forgive me for being blunt. Micromanagement means a leader does not trust subordinates to make good decisions. Why? Because the leader is so fearful of mistakes, he or she is afraid to trust others.

Fearful leaders transfer their fear to the rest of the organization. This always results in subordinates being afraid to make decisions. Micromanaged subordinates can be so worried about the boss's reaction that they never take risks. Lack of risk-taking results in mediocrity.

Micromanagement is also destructive because no one person is smart enough to always make the best decision. Each of us has blind spots and preconceived ideas that sometimes shade our perceptions. The only way to prevent this is to make sure some of the people in our inner circle are willing and able to present contrarian views.

I once ran a station in which the chief engineer often played the role of contrarian. It would not be unusual during a department head meeting for the chief to quietly listen to a discussion run its course, then suddenly insert a left-field idea. This drove some of the other department heads crazy. After all, we were in agreement with each other. Why was this guy causing trouble? What they didn't know was that in private, I had urged the chief engineer to play this role. He had a rare blend of creativity and practicality that was unhampered by a need to fit in. His ideas were not always accepted, but on many occasions, he made the group's idea better. He also saved us from disaster more than once by simply pointing out potholes the rest of us overlooked.

If micromanaging is a mistake, what is the right approach? There is no single answer, but I am in the camp of those who say pushing business decisions to the lowest level is one secret to a great organization. The people closest to the decision are usually the ones with the most information and in the best position to make the right call. The risk of this approach is that people sometimes make mistakes.

If you are unwilling to accept mistakes, then become a micromanager. Just remember, you have to be right all the time.

Renewing Your Personal Goals

I spent the first nineteen years of my career wanting to become a general manager. When I achieved that goal, I suddenly found myself at loose ends. What now? I eventually decided I wanted to run a major-market station. After achieving that goal, I wanted to run a top-ten station. After that, the fun seemed to go out of it until I realized what really made me happy was taking a station from last to first. Having worked for a great number of poor leaders, I also wanted to help new general managers avoid some of the mistakes I had made. Those goals became my career drivers while running stations and simultaneously working at Northwestern University's Media Management Center. Those pursuits have been more satisfying than anything else in my career.

Many general managers believe their natural next step is to the corporate level. A corporate job was tempting but not something I dreamed of. I loved the energy and direct contact only a station could bring. I also loved the idea of inventing the future, making a local television station become something far more important: a brand that actually dominates local news and information, no matter what the platform. For that to happen, our industry needed leaders far better equipped than my generation. Helping equip those leaders continues to drive me now.

There are any number of successful general managers who are not only focused on the long-term future of their stations but plan to lead their stations for the rest of their careers. Their commitment extends to the communities they live in. Those are also worthy goals, just not mine. I love the thrill of the chase from last to first.

As you think about your personal career goals, try to look beyond what you are doing now. If possible, try to look multiple steps down the road. As you travel on your journey, your goals may well change. Experience has a way of doing that. What's important is that you never become someone who is merely putting in time or waiting for retirement. You will not only find yourself unhappy, you will be denying those who report to you their chance to excel.

Above all, find out what you love and do it! I know that sounds trite, but it is no less true.

Understanding your motivations, the motivations of others, and the best interests of the organization you lead combine to give you not only a foundation for success but also a foundation to begin a broader, multidimensional understanding of our industry—what is often called the big picture.

Understanding the Big Picture

I once worked with a sales manager who was renowned for training new account executives. Time after time, she had helped young people become successful sellers. Unfortunately, that skill set did not transfer well into the general sales manager role. On the face of it, she should have been a great leader because of her developmental skills, but she was not. One day, she came into my office and said, "You are always talking about 'the big picture.' Can you show it to me?" She thought the big picture was a document. I realized then what the problem was. She was a trainer, not a leader. She could not see beyond the details.

Let me explain. Leaders must have the ability to not only see the ultimate goals but also keep their organization's activities on track to reach those goals. Understanding the big picture is seeing how all these activities fit together to achieve a final result. Mastering that level of understanding gives you the ability to then realize which activities are important and which simply waste resources.

Understanding the big picture is critical because it provides a standard of measurement for everything you do. If an activity does not fit into the big picture, why do it? It also helps delineate the difference between strategy and tactics. Strategy is for the long term, carefully thought out so that it always remains in place. Tactics are activities that advance a strategy. By their nature, tactics can change with market conditions. A strategy that changes with market conditions is not really a strategy at all.

One way to understand the big picture is to simply stop and think about it. Most people in our industry never take the time to think. They are much more comfortable following whatever patterns and rules have been established in the past. Making your station look like all others is an easy path many take. It requires no understanding of bigger things. You simply do whatever everyone else does.

How important is understanding the big picture? In virtually every television market, one will find at least one television station that appears to do a good job yet produces mediocre results. Look closely and you will usually see a station that is so homogenized, so locked into conventional industry thinking, that nothing distinguishes it. Those organizations are usually led by general managers who, although successful on other levels, do not understand the big picture.

Organizational Focus

We will discuss creating a strategic plan in a later chapter, but for now, let's talk about how a leader helps an organization focus on strategic goals.

Micromanagers do not require an organization to focus. The organization simply does whatever the manager instructs it to do. Focus is the micromanager's job. The micromanager is always right.

Since I've never been smart enough to be right all the time, I've had to find ways to keep everyone focused on the same priorities, reaching for the same goals. Making sure everyone understands the station's strategy sounds simple. It is not.

I've tried everything. Signs around the building are helpful, as are quarterly staff meetings, but the strongest tool, at least for me, is to constantly work the station's ultimate goals and strategy for achieving them into everyday conversation.

Focus is especially important because a station always needs new, creative ideas to advance its agenda. Unfortunately, creativity can be the enemy of focus because it can easily veer a station off track. Creativity is only effective when it too focuses on the station's strategy.

How do you communicate strategy to your staff? I talk about our strategy and goals wherever I go. To clients, members of the community, anyone I talk to. "But wait," you might say. "Doesn't this expose your strategy to competitors?" Yes, it does, but I have two answers. First, if we hide our strategy from our competitors, it will also be hidden from our own staff. Second, a strategy that is easily copied by competitors is not a strategy at all.

Commander's Intent

Anyone who has spent a day at the US Army War College in Pennsylvania understands the concept of commander's intent. Totalitarian countries usually have top-down control of their military forces. All decisions, including tactical changes during the middle of battle, are made at that level.

The United States Army does not function that way. Battlefield decisions are made by captains and lieutenants, who are empowered to make decisions on the ground. They make those decisions based on an understanding of their commander's intent. That frees them to take command, making whatever decisions they believe are right. The ability to act based on commander's intent, as opposed to micromanagement by the commander, is one of the army's greatest strengths.

As a general manager, you can also use commander's intent to successfully run your station. Your job is to focus everyone on station goals. Helping them understand the big picture and the strategy for achieving goals gives them an understanding of commander's intent, creating a powerful tool for decision-making on all levels. Not every decision they make will be the right one, but neither will yours.

The Peril of Uniformity

One of the most frustrating things about television is the sameness that seems to permeate every affiliated station in the country. Some of this is due to the prevalence of news consultants, the most famous of which is Frank N. Magid Associates. Having been one of Frank's team of young people who thought they knew everything back in the day, I have to take some blame for this, but the fact is most stations look and feel pretty much the same as their competitors.

If you are the general manager of the number-one station in a market, then more power to you. You benefit from everyone else trying to be like you. Forget the competition and figure out how to advance your winning brand. But what about the second-, third-, and fourth-place stations? Why do they all seem to look and feel the same?

The answer is in human nature. People want to experience the comfort of feeling they are doing things the "right" way. They want to know the rules, so they look to the market leader to model those rules. Rarely does anyone ask why. They simply accept the idea that news is done a certain way. Once they understand the rules, they are reluctant to ever make changes.

For instance, why do we have reporter live shots and packages? Not because those things necessarily advance the story or benefit the viewer but because they are vehicles to put the reporter on television. Don't believe me? Go to any morning meeting in any newsroom and listen. Reporters all want to know, "What's my package? What's my live shot?" Try telling a reporter you are reducing the number of packages and see what happens. I've done it, and the response is not pretty.

Why do some stations put the time on the screen during evening newscasts? Because other stations do it. Putting the time on the screen during the morning is a good idea because people are getting ready to leave for work or school. Putting the time up in a late newscast makes no sense because it reminds people it is time to go to bed. That's why casinos have no clocks.

Why do most stations do sweep stories even though they rarely work? Because every other station does sweep stories.

Why is news done at a desk with two anchors, one sports person, and one weatherperson? Because that's the way we do news. And speaking of weather people, why is the main one always the chief meteorologist?

I'm not suggesting you make wholesale changes to your newscasts. In fact, wholesale change is a bad idea because it upsets viewers. I am suggesting you can gain an advantage simply by doing the one thing most of your competitors will never do: asking why. Being willing to ask questions and learn is the mark of a confident leader.

Leading Your Competitors

Your ability to lead is not limited to your own station.

Many years ago, I was the production manager at WPEC, the then–ABC affiliate in West Palm Beach. Our station was always in second place to WPTV, the NBC affiliate.

Walking through the halls of WPEC, one seemed to always be hearing about WPTV. Usually the conversation involved reasons why we could never seem to beat them in the ratings. One constant refrain was, "They are owned by a big company that will spend anything to win. They have more people and better equipment. They pay better. No matter what we do, they have the money to do it better."

The news ratings at WPEC finally got so bad the owner decided to do away with production and concentrate all his resources on news. I lost my job. With a pregnant wife, one child, and no money, I was desperate, so I called Bob Regalbuto, the GM of WPTV, and asked for an appointment. Regalbuto not only saw me, but hired me as promotion manager.

Working at WPTV was a revelation. The station had about the same size staff as WPEC. Most equipment and facilities were pretty much the same. Far from being willing to spend anything, money was very tight. None of the things I had heard was true, yet WPTV dominated news ratings while WPEC came in a distant second.

The difference was leadership. Regalbuto had not only created a winning atmosphere at his station; he had convinced his competitors they could not beat him. He had done this in part by making sure his staff knew they were winners who set the market agenda. Their overriding sense of leadership became obvious anytime they dealt with the staff from WPEC, especially when news crews ran into each other covering stories. As a result, WPEC's staff constantly sought excuses for their inferiority. The more they talked about WPTV, the greater their inferiority became.

By making WPTV their standard for success, WPEC could never win. Bob Regalbuto was setting the agenda for both stations.

The WPTV-WPEC analogy was not unique to West Palm Beach. Staffs of leading stations believe they can win because that message is constantly being reinforced by their leadership. Failing stations invariably focus on the leading station's agenda, which automatically means they cannot win.

If you are a second- or third-place station that wants to be number one, you are far better off concentrating on your own strategy rather than talking about what another station does. Admittedly, this is hard to do, but concentrating on someone else's strategy automatically puts you behind the curve, allowing a competitor to set the agenda for your station.

Having spent a good part of my career doing turnarounds, I would never begin a new project by using the current number-one station as a standard for success. They are the people we are eventually going to beat using our strategy and executing our game plan, not theirs. Why in the world would you see them as the standard?

I'm not saying you should be unaware of competitor strengths and weaknesses, but concentrating on beating someone else at their own game is always a bad idea. If that's the best you can do, then good luck. You will need it.

Celebrating Mistakes

If you attend enough company meetings, sooner or later you may hear the mantra, "We celebrate our mistakes." I wish that were true. No one celebrates mistakes. The better question is, "Do we learn from our mistakes?"

People who report to you are going to make mistakes. Some are little mistakes you accept because they are a learning experience for the managers, but others are consequential. Both are going to happen, so it is worth taking the time to learn from them.

When solid performers make mistakes, they are the first to beat themselves up, so it is counterproductive for you to pile on. Don't minimize the importance of the mistake, but make sure the person knows you understand and that it will be used as a learning experience and will not happen again.

Of course, some mistakes, such as financial impropriety, grossly inappropriate behavior, or lying, are not fixable. When that happens, move quickly toward separation because those kinds of mistakes cannot be tolerated.

Creating Other Leaders

Great organizations always have effective leaders on multiple levels. Certainly, the general manager sets the tone, but effective leadership always reaches down to other levels in the organization.

Part of your responsibility as the organization's leader is to create those other great leaders. Earlier in this chapter, we talked about the advantages of pushing decision-making to the lowest level. Decision-making and leadership go hand in hand.

As the leader, department heads and other employees are constantly asking you to make decisions. "What should I do about . . . ?" is a common question. These are great opportunities to teach leadership.

My answer is usually "What do you think?" I've learned over the years that once I express an opinion, it becomes difficult for the employee to express a different opinion. Far better to hear from that person first. For the most part, they already know the answer to the question, and they usually have the best solution. They are coming to you seeking validation. Unless you ask what they think, the best solution may never come up simply because you have already closed the door by expressing a contrary opinion. By asking what they think, you are helping them learn to have confidence in their decision-making ability. You are also modeling what leadership looks like.

Making decisions, and having those decisions confirmed, is a positive starting point for the kind of self-confidence leadership requires. One of the great pleasures you will enjoy as the group's leader is seeing other people develop their own leadership skills.

Let's assume you have identified a person on your staff that is exhibiting initiative, good judgment, and other positive characteristics of a future leader. You owe it to that person, as well as the company you work for, to aid in the person's development. One of the best ways to do that is to spend time mentoring.

Two important words of caution. First, make sure you are not selecting someone simply because you are comfortable with him or her. It is easy to choose people who are "just like you." Far better to choose people based on their skills, desire, and willingness to learn.

The second caution is to beware of too close a relationship. Any actions, innuendos, or overtones that might be construed as sexual are off-limits. These are professional relationships, not personal. Reasonable boundaries are important. For instance, dinner with just the two of you might be a bad idea. Anything having to do with alcohol is also dangerous. Your guard must always be up, both for your sake and the sake of the other person.

There is a massive power difference between you and the person you are mentoring. Never engage in behavior that might call your professional intent into question. It is not worth the consequences to you, your family, and your career.

Summary

At its core, leadership is about helping an organization achieve important goals by working through others. Great leaders understand that they do not have all the answers. What they do have is the ability to clearly articulate a vision that others buy into.

Leaders define goals, making sure every employee knows what those goals are and the part each person plays. The best leaders also understand they will only be successful if the people who report to them are also successful.

Leadership style is not something that just happens. It is the result of being able to see the endgame and how to get there, supported by the hard work of keeping others on track to that same endgame.

Great leaders have self-perspective, see the big picture, understand that the office they hold offers both advantages and barriers to success, are willing to sometimes put personal rewards aside in order to achieve unity in the organization, seek authenticity in their dealings with staff members on all levels, and above all, recognize that success is always a group effort.

Key Takeaways

- Leaders are always the key players in a company's success or failure.
- Understanding how employees see leaders is the first step toward using the power of leadership to create a great organization.
- Great leaders have the ability to motivate employees to believe in a vision.
- Understanding your own motivation helps you motivate others.
- How an organization wins always matters.
- Putting potential failure into perspective lessens the fear of failure.
- Transparency and authenticity are essential tools of great leaders.
- Great leaders always work through others.
- Micromanagers not only lose the benefit of better ideas but also have to be right all the time.

- Understanding the big picture helps to direct focus.
- Great leaders sometimes lead not only their own stations but also their competitors' stations.
- You have an obligation to not only lead but also create other great leaders.

3

THE POWER OF CONTENT

How many times have you heard someone say, "Things are changing so fast that it's hard to know what the future will bring"? Over the years, I've heard that statement from managers and leaders at all levels. Is it true? Is change happening too rapidly to know what the future will bring?

During my fifteen years at the Media Management Center, much of my time was spent trying to understand the future. Are we simply at the mercy of new technology and other disruptions, or is there a bigger picture we can understand? Is experience still valuable, or does the new world only belong to the very young? While no one can fully see the future, there is some good news. The current evolution in media is part of a logical progression and therefore, to some degree, predictive. Technology is constantly changing, and the world of media will continue to fragment, but by understanding the sociological forces at work, we can begin to properly frame technological innovations, giving us a way to make some broad sense of the future.

What cannot be predicted is disruptive innovation. But remember, innovation only has value if it also has consumer support. Apple did not invent the tablet. The iPad succeeded where others failed because it gained massive consumer support. When disruptive innovation does happen, taking the time to understand why it happened can give us valuable competitive advantages.

Technology frightens us because we make the mistake of thinking we are in the television technology business. We are not. Television is our primary form of distribution, not the core of our business. Our business is creating local content, supplemented by national content we gather from others. We make money by charging advertisers for access to the end users of our content. We also make money by charging the consumer to access our content. This is done through a distribution agent, such as cable.

Why Content Matters

A little over five hundred years ago, in 1517, an obscure German monk named Martin Luther found himself at odds with the established church regarding a number of issues, most notably the authority of the Bible and the selling of indulgences.

Luther felt so strongly about these issues that he decided to use the media to go public, taking a stand that would put his life at risk. But how could he do this? His answer was to write what he called his Ninety-Five Theses on a parchment, which he then nailed to the church door in the public square. Why nail it to the church door? Because that was the primary form of mass media in the sixteenth century. Within six months, his theses had been copied and translated into every European language. Luther is still being read today.

From Luther, we learn the first and most important lesson of media: the power is in the content, not the technology.

Why Technology Matters

Let's now move forward from 1517 to 1776. The British colonies in America were in a tax revolt that had already become bloody. The revolt did not start as a call for independence. Colonists saw themselves as British citizens. "No taxation without representation" was a demand to be treated the same as their English cousins.

Within this movement was a group of radicals who were not content with the idea of equal treatment. They wanted to "throw off the yoke" of British domination and create an entirely new nation. But they were the radicals, not yet the mainstream. How could they convince fellow subjects that the time for independence was at hand?

The answer came from a young man named Thomas Paine. Paine decided to put his radical ideas on paper and, like Luther, use mass media to disseminate his message. Unlike Luther, Paine was not willing to risk his neck, so he decided to publish anonymously. Like Luther, he decided to use the latest technology.

Newspapers existed in 1776, but publishing such a document would be treason. Plus, there was no way to share information from newspaper to newspaper–no Associated Press. Finally, there was the problem of concealing his identity.

Paine's answer was to publish his ideas in a pamphlet he titled *Common Sense*. Paine's words struck a chord. Copies were handed from person to person across the colonies until *Common Sense* became part of the lexicon. It was one of the reasons that, on July 4 of that same year, the colonists issued a Declaration of Independence. A tax revolt had turned into secession.

From Thomas Paine, we learn the second great lesson of media: content always gravitates toward the latest technology.

In the 1850s, Harriet Beecher Stowe used a novel to expose the evils of slavery. In the 1930s, Franklin Roosevelt used network radio to calm a nation during the Great Depression. In the 1960s, Martin Luther King Jr. used network television to drive the civil rights movement.

Content always gravitates toward the latest technology, which is why 78 RPM records became stereo hi-fi, why hi-fi became CDs, why CDs became MP3 players, why MP3 players became streaming music services, and why streaming music services are not the last word.

These two truisms—the power is in the content and content always gravitates to the latest technology—are baselines for understanding the future of media.

Think about the early days of television. People with new sets would watch anything just for the experience, but that early phase quickly wore off because technology without content is meaningless. Had the networks not quickly begun to produce watchable programming, television would be only a curious footnote in history.

Content and Technology Are Bound by Culture

Every organization, every endeavor, every group of people with shared values has a culture. Culture is essential because it frames our conversations, making sense of the things we do. It is a powerful force that is present in every aspect of our lives. If you want to find out how powerful, just try to change it.

For instance, our television culture says that evening local newscasts should have three parts: news, weather, and sports, always in that order. What happens if you eliminate sports? The earth shakes, viewers complain, and the newsroom thinks you have lost your mind. We have been doing newscasts this way for so many decades, we've conditioned both viewers and ourselves to believe any other way is illegitimate.

New technology threatens our television culture because it does not follow the established norms, which makes us wary and uncomfortable. Moreover, there is pressure from older viewers to not change anything. Our usual answer is the worst one possible. We try to add new things without taking anything old away. As a result, we have accepted the idea that younger viewers are not interested in television news and will only use products that are on demand and likely mobile-based. We have taken the easy way out, writing off the future of linear television news viewing. But does it have to be this way? Can we innovate without killing our current business model?

To answer that question, we must start by understanding the cultures that drive media organizations. Why are we competitive by nature? Why are our organizations inwardly directed? Why do we never change any of the basics while still buying into every fad our competitors put on the air? Why do we believe the things we believe and do the things we do?

Let's begin about a hundred years ago, at a time when newspapers dominated media.

Thanks to the First Amendment, by the early twentieth century, newspapers represented a wide variety of ideas and positions. In Chicago alone, there were forty daily newspapers by 1925. Some were in foreign languages, and some had specialized content, but that left a wide range of daily general interest papers. As anyone who has watched *The Front Page* or *His Girl Friday* knows, newspapers were highly competitive.

Newspapers also took positions. That's why some had names like the *Democrat* or the *Independent*. The idea that there were two sides of a story was not necessarily the norm in those days.

Running a newspaper was not an easy business, but it was exciting and creative. Reading a biography of Hearst or Pulitzer opens a window on a competitive age that no longer exists. So what happened?

The great newspapers in those days were afternoon dailies. They were read after work and dinner. Morning newspapers were also popular but less powerful.

The first crack in the power of newspapers was the advent of network radio, not because radio was a competitor for news but because prime-time radio used up some of the time consumers had previously used to read newspapers.

When television came along after World War II, it was only natural that the competitiveness of newspapers would cause them to apply for television station licenses. At a time when television made no money and very few consumers could afford sets, newspaper owners had the foresight to understand television was the next big competitive game. They built stations, hired staff, and created local programming—all at a loss, ensuring that new technology would not leave them in the dust. That took guts.

As television caught on and viewers began to spend a significant amount of time at their sets, they had less time to read afternoon papers, which eventually led to newspaper consolidation. Strong papers bought weak ones and absorbed them.

The game changer came on November 22, 1963, the day I believe modern television news was invented.

The assassination of President John F. Kennedy brought American life to a screeching halt. People rushed home and turned on their televisions. For the next three days, the entire nation was glued to either CBS or NBC, often flipping between them.

Looking at tapes of the Kennedy assassination coverage, one is struck not only by the drama of the event but by the creation of a new form of mass communication right before the viewers' eyes. In living rooms across the nation, viewers were witness to the events as they unfolded live. Everything television news was to become in the future had its roots in those few days. By the following Monday, an enduring bond had been created between the viewers and this revolutionary new medium.

Up until that time, television news was a headline service. For the most part, it was not even profitable. Overnight viewers began to see television news in a different way, as a medium with unique strengths that were very different from a printed page.

By the 1970s, local television news was a profitable enterprise. By the end of that decade, afternoon newspapers were dead.

The death of afternoon papers accelerated the consolidation of morning papers in a way no one expected. By the early 1980s, most markets were down to one newspaper. That fact completely changed the way newspapers thought about themselves and how they operated. Instead of a competitive business, newspapers were now a monopoly, not unlike the power company or a public utility. They began to see themselves as part of the public trust.

Newspapers also became very profitable. Without competition, newspapers were able to raise advertising and subscription prices, especially for small mom-and-pop retailers who had no other options. Large advertisers, like auto dealers, were required to sign annual contracts. To not do so was to pay an even higher rate every time they bought an individual ad.

The profitability of newspapers did not necessarily translate into higher wages for their employees. On the contrary, with no other papers to bid up the price, salaries began to drop, especially after the large chains started to grow. This caused dissention within employee ranks. Newspapers were now big businesses, beholden more to stockholders than readers. Over time, journalism schools began to reflect the new reality of newspapers. Since there were no competing newspapers in most communities, the question of fair reporting arose. The discussion of journalistic ethics became much more prominent.

The biggest change was in attitude. Previously, publishers had come from the editorial or sales ranks. As the mission of newspapers changed, so did leadership. It became much more about management than enterprise. Salespeople still became publishers but so did circulation managers and even human resource managers.

The practical result was that newspapers lost their accountability to readers. Formulaic reporting grew. Editorial writers were free to be at odds with the communities they served, knowing there would be no economic backlash. Because many writers were poorly paid, editorial content began to shift left.

No one consciously tried to make these things happen. They were the natural result of monopolization.

By the 1990s, newspaper profits were at all-time highs. It was not unusual for a large metro newspaper's ad revenue to be as much as all market television stations combined. Profit margins were lower than television stations, but actual profits were much higher.

Back in the 1940s, newspapers were the first to invest in television; but when the internet became a real force, newspapers were never really in the game. Early on, many papers experimented with digital but soon found there was no immediate money to be made and cut back their investments.

If newspapers had followed the formula that worked so well for them during the invention of television, they would likely have ended up dominating news and information on the web. It would have been expensive and time consuming, but it would have morphed their industry into something entirely new. Instead, they treated the web as illegitimate, a form of media that was "stealing" newspaper content and giving it away for free.

What are the big-picture lessons those of us in television can learn from newspapers? I suggest the following.

Newspapers were destined to fail because they could not make the cultural leap from believing their strength was their distribution system to understanding their real strength was content. They also failed to understand that the migration of content to a better technology was not an illegitimate use of content.

The appeal of owning the distribution system blinded newspapers to the reality that people read the paper because of what was in it, not because it was printed on paper. If that meant having to go outside every morning and find the paper, they were willing to do it. But the minute a more convenient technology came along, readers did not hesitate to make the change. This is a classic case of industry culture being stronger than reality. Newspapers could not transition to a new platform because they believed their power was in their technology, not their content.

One must also take into account the inverse relationship between profitability and risk. The higher the profitability, the less appetite for risk. It is one thing to look back and say that at the height of their profitability, newspapers should have invested heavily in brand extension to a new platform. It would be quite another for any of us in the same shoes at the same time to not do the same thing they did.

All of this begs the question, Is local television headed down the same road? Not exactly. Many of the perils for television are the same as newspapers, but television has the advantage of still living in a competitive world. The 2008/2009 advertising recession removed much of our arrogance, but even now we still think of ourselves as "just television," when we are actually so much more. The lesson of newspapers is for us to take full advantage of new opportunities while our traditional platforms are still strong enough to be building blocks to the future.

What Makes New Technology Valuable

Apple did not invent tablets, but they did make tablets a required household item. Apple succeeded where others failed because they also invented a convenient way for tablets to deliver content. Without the invention of apps, which they had already begun to develop on the iPhone, the iPad would have failed. Apps were important because they provided unique content to the consumer in easy-to-use, targeted bites. Access to content was the real value.

New technology only has value if the consumer chooses to use it. A number of years ago, television set manufacturers saw 3-D pictures as the new rage. Every high-end set seemed to also offer 3-D. Viewers took a look at 3-D, were not enamored by the picture or the fact that they had to wear special glasses, and rejected it.

Technology only has value if consumers choose to use it.

Old Technology versus New Technology

Thinking of technology as "old versus new" is a mistake. Instead, think of appropriate technology for a particular consumer need.

If a person is sitting in an office and gets a weather alert, that alert will most likely come from her smartphone, which is the most appropriate technology for alerts because it is always with the consumer. Upon seeing the alert, she may call up the station's website on her computer because the weather map will be larger and easier to read. When she gets home, she will likely turn on her television because the picture will be both larger and of higher quality. She chooses each of these devices because it is the most appropriate one for her need at a current time and place.

The weather alert example also proves another truism. Quality only comes into play when content is equal. Because the only way to access a weather alert was on her phone, the viewer was glued to it. But once she arrived home, she chose her big-screen TV because the quality was better.

Movie theaters are a technology in long-term decline, yet people still go to the movies. Why? The answer is that theaters offer a social experience, someplace to go on a night out. Most of the time, consumers watch movies at home on their big-screen TVs, but on some occasions, a movie theater is the more appropriate vehicle for content because of the social factor.

Print is the oldest technology of all but still has great value. A person might choose a paperback book to carry on a trip rather than risk leaving his or her iPad on an airplane. A high gloss magazine can sometimes be more enjoyable than an app.

Because the latest content always moves to the latest technology, the use of older technologies will continually change. Many will be marginalized and some eliminated not because they are old but because they are no longer the most appropriate platform for certain content. Recall that 78 RPM records were replaced by LPs. LPs were replaced by CDs, which were in turn replaced by streaming music services. Each move was logical because the next technology made content available either at higher quality or more conveniently. However, LPs are back in vogue as a niche product for audiophiles who prefer the waves of analog sound to the numeric bits of digital. Old or new is not the question. The question is what technology is most appropriate to deliver a particular experience to the consumer.

Understanding appropriate content is important groundwork for building the future of local television.

The Television Opportunity

Television is in a unique time. News ratings continue to decline, and there are far too many players in the local news business. That is balanced for the moment by the fact that local television is the last form of mass media. If you want to sell cars, create consumer traffic, or get elected to a national office, you pretty much have to advertise on television.

In addition to ad revenue, stations now get real money from retransmission payments. Sure, networks take a large bite, but that just ensures networks have the resources to continue providing top-tier entertainment.

Local news audiences continue to age, but during an emergency or major breaking news, consumers of all ages turn to local television first. With the demise of local newspapers, television has become an essential medium for local information. Ask any cable, satellite, or over-the-top (OTT) provider if their business model works without carriage of local stations.

Looking forward, ATSC 3.0 and other innovations continue to breathe new life into an old medium. One can argue that ATSC 3.0 and its successors with integrated 5G and other two-way communication are actually new platforms, yet ATSC 3.0 is embraceable because we think of it as television.

Does all this mean local television is not at risk? Of course not. Ratings and viewer age are the writing on the wall. We either have to find ways to attract younger viewers to a linear experience, or we must change platforms to reflect current viewer preferences. History says viewer preferences will win out. There is a place for linear viewing in the future, but it will be one platform among many others. How that eventually looks does not matter. What matters is that you own the strongest local content brand.

We cannot talk about the power of content without also acknowledging there are simply too many players in most markets competing for the same end users of the same content. Eventually, the excess of local news, the unprecedented level of industry debt, and a future recession will force bottom players out.

So what about the stations that are left? They have the opportunity to morph into something that will eventually become far more important and far more financially rewarding than anything in the past: a dominant local news brand.

In addition to the things we have discussed, consider the following:

• As the last form of mass media, leading television stations are massive launchpads, able to introduce new ideas and services to all age consumers.

• Local television stations have an existing relationship with consumers. Viewers see this relationship in personal terms of trust and reliability. This is especially important in a time when consumer trust of national media is diminishing.

• Stations are powerful forces in their communities. Look what happens when a leading station gets behind a community event.

- Because of their news-gathering role, stations have unique resources unavailable to any other form of local media.
- By nature, television people are highly competitive. The best hate to lose. Whatever shape the future takes, it will certainly be competitive.

How do we take these powerful attributes and use them to invent the future? Those with a broad user base, the ability to create strong local content, and financial stability for the long run will be able to convert from platform-based businesses to brand-based businesses. This does not mean they will stop being in the television business. It means television will simply be one way, among many others, they connect with local consumers.

None of us knows what technology the future will bring, but we do know this: new technology will continue to be introduced and will continue to disrupt the business models of old technology. Some new technology will result in incredible changes in the way consumers connect with media and each other. Many more forms of technology will be introduced but quickly fail. Which technology is accepted and which is rejected is entirely up to the consumer.

The good news is television stations do not have to predict which platforms the consumer will choose in the future. They only have to be prepared to immediately extend their brands to follow viewer choices.

Brand Is the Key

Because we see the world through the lens of our current culture, anything that materially changes the status quo of that culture is seen as a threat. Thus, our first reaction to new forms of distribution is defensive. The vestiges of a gatekeeper make it even more difficult for us to accept new technology that gives the consumer an active voice in content decisions or production.

Does this mean we are bound by our culture? It does if we accept the status quo, something most media companies continue to do. However, for the few who are willing to go through the difficult process of looking at the world through an objective lens, changing the status quo becomes a compelling competitive opportunity.

At its core, brand is simply a way of looking at reality in the same way as consumers. Understanding that reality is the first step toward future success.

Summary

The power of media is always in the content. Technology is merely a way to disseminate content.

Content always moves to the latest technology. That does not mean old platforms no longer have value. Instead, we should think in terms of appropriate technology.

How content and technology work together is determined by our culture. Culture limits the way we see the world, causing us to miss what should be obvious opportunities. Because culture develops over long periods of time, it is always difficult to change.

Television news suffers from too much uniformity, meaning the marketplace will eventually force some weak players out. That does not mean stronger players do not have to change. Evolution by strong players works. Revolution by weaker players always fails.

The future is bright for companies that create dominant local news brands.

Key Takeaways

- **Content is the core value of any media company.**
- **Content always gravitates to the latest technology.**

- Content and technology are seen through the lens of internal culture, making new technology appear to be a threat.
- The evolution of media is part of a logical progression based on consumer needs and interests.
- Consumers are in charge of the future.
- New technology only has value when consumers choose to use it.
- Thinking of a media company in terms of brand instead of platform is a way of overcoming our internal culture in order to deal with reality.
- Those who possess a market's dominant local news brand have a future even brighter than anything in the past.

4

The Power of Brand

Positioning

Back in 1981, Al Ries and Jack Trout wrote a groundbreaking book called *Positioning: The Battle for Your Mind.* Their premise was that because consumers live in a world full of choices, they need a way to short-cut decisions. As a result, consumers assign "positions" to products and services. A Mercedes-Benz might be "the car that impresses people." Hellmann's mayonnaise might "taste better than the others." Once established, positions are hard to change.

Ries and Trout believed that every product or service had a position in the consumer's mind. If one could adjust the consumer's perception of a product, buying choices would be affected. "Positioning" was an early description of what we now call brand.

When *Positioning: The Battle for Your Mind* came out, Jim Ellis and I were young consultants for Frank Magid and traveled the country touting the value of positioning. Many stations were already using slogans such as "11 Alive" or "9 Strong" in their advertising, but those were mainly to get attention. Slogans were designed to make a station stand out from the crowd, not actually influence viewer behavior.

Positioning caught on like a firestorm. Ours is a copycat business, so when one station in a market took a "position," every other station had to have one too. This was the era before fragmentation, so stations' competitors were for the most part just other stations. There was also some evidence that positioning could work. Since the 1970s, KCRA in Sacramento had been calling themselves the station "Where the News Comes First." KCRA was one of the highest-rated stations in the country. Their commitment to local news coverage was unequaled. At KCRA, the news really did come first. It was a great example of advertising based on genuine product strengths.

The problem with positioning was that the positioning lines were often unrealistic. To be effective, a line had to offer viewers a genuine reason to watch, based on true strengths of the station. Too often, lines were chosen because they sounded good. I was guilty of this myself in 1983 at WJLA in Washington, DC. The station at that time was in third place, with not much hope of beating the market-leading CBS and NBC stations. Research showed WJLA's only real strength was a consumer segment fronted by reporter Paul Berry called "On Your Side." Thus was born "7 On Your Side."

With nothing better to choose from, station manager Dow Smith and I, along with legendary marketing consultant Bob Klein, spent $500,000 (1983 dollars) on a multimedia campaign. We hired Tom Scott to write the music, which we recorded in London. Jeffrey Osborne did the vocals. Spots were shot in 35 mm using a top director and postproduction company. The campaign was a beautiful thing to behold. Bob Klein syndicated the idea to stations across the country, many of which still use the line today. The result on WJLA's ratings: no movement.

The problem with "On Your Side" was twofold. First, did viewers really believe we were on their side? More importantly, just how would this motivate them to switch from their favorite newscast to ours? This is not to say "On Your Side" could not work somewhere else. In WJLA's case, it simply did not motivate viewers, something we should have known at the outset. Why did we do it? The honest answer is that it was creative, the music sounded great, and it won awards.

Some positioning lines actually worked. KSL in Salt Lake City created a campaign called the News Specialists, based on their beat system of reporting. By assigning individual reporters to beats, KSL made the claim that viewers received an advantage when news was reported by local specialists.

There are, of course, other successful cases, but for the most part, positions were simply slogans by another name.

Most stations were smart enough to realize their positions had to be explained in marketing and reinforced in product. Marketing was easy. Product was hard. How do you fulfill a positioning promise when your content is so similar to everyone else's? Lacking a better answer, stations instructed their reporters to tag stories with the station's positioning line: "Mary Jones, WXXX, Content You Can Count On."

Did positioning lines work? For the most part, no. They were often contrived devices based on nothing more than a perceived void in the market. Only when the lines offered a unique viewer benefit, based on actual content, did positioning work.

Branding

Let's fast-forward to the early twenty-first century. Cable, satellite, and internet had created a fragmented world offering viewers a wide range of media choices. But more media was only part of the problem. Viewers had an ever-widening range of other activities, and anything that took up a consumer's time was now a competitor.

As stations began to grapple with this new world, positioning was suddenly out and branding was in. What was the difference between positioning and branding? Not much. One term was replaced with another. Instead of talking about "our position," stations started talking about "our brand."

The problem with both position and brand (at least the way our industry uses the terms) is that both are usually based on internal station desires, not true unique viewer benefits. They look nice, sound nice, and coordinate a station's look. Rarely do they also motivate viewers.

For instance, take the phrase "Coverage You Can Count On." Does that mean other stations have coverage viewers cannot count on? Do viewers really believe they can count on a station they do not normally watch more than their longtime favorite? What does "count on" really mean anyway? There are no doubt stations where the line makes sense because of local market conditions. If the line actually describes a unique consumer benefit your station offers, then by all means use it. Just make sure you have thought it out.

Consider the process most stations use to determine their brand. It starts with market research. Viewers are asked about their lives, viewing patterns, and favorite stations. The researcher typically presents a wide range of newscast attributes, such as breaking news, emergency weather, health news, education news, and so on. Viewers are asked to rank the importance of each attribute. They are then asked which local stations do the best job of fulfilling those attributes.

The result is that the researcher discovers market voids. Let's say consumers in a particular market express a strong interest in investigative reporting yet do not think any station does a particularly good job in this area. "Aha!" says the researcher. "We have discovered a void in the market!"

The researcher then suggests that their client make investigative reporting a priority. The station buys into the idea and chooses the slogan "The Investigators." A brand is born.

In the coming weeks, the station begins to do regular in-depth stories they label "investigations." Every story by any reporter, whether it be investigative or not, ends with "Tom Smith, Channel 9, the Investigators."

What is wrong with this process? It's based on research, fills a perceived viewer need, and distinguishes the station. Those are good things. Here's the problem. Viewers choose a favorite station for a wide variety of reasons and do this over time. They reject other stations for those same reasons. Is an emphasis on "investigations" enough to change other viewer perceptions? Even done well, does that one element trump everything else? If everything else is equal, then possibly yes. But everything else is not equal.

Stations often claim success for their brands by pointing to later research showing viewers associate that brand with their station. That's fine, as far as it goes, but association is not the question. The real question is, has the brand changed viewer behavior? The answer to that can only be measured by actual ratings. Unfortunately, stations are rarely able to tie their brands directly to ratings success.

Creating and maintaining a brand image is expensive and takes hard work, so we are naturally inclined to believe in our brands, but how effective is that work? There are a number of notable success stories where branding lines are helpful. But for the average station in third or fourth place, their brand rarely adds value. This begs the question, Why are branding lines not more effective?

To begin with, most brands do not offer unique consumer benefits. When a station says, "Local First," do viewers think other stations do not put local first? If a station says, "Committed to You," do the consumers actually believe the station is "committed" to them? Do they believe one station is more committed than other stations in the same market?

On the other hand, a station that does a better job of live coverage, provides more local information, and owns breaking news might successfully use the line "Live, Local, and Late Breaking." But the line only works if viewers agree those are unique benefits provided by that particular station.

For the most part, branding lines are simply taglines stations hope in some unmeasurable way will increase viewer loyalty. In practice, most branding lines are just wallpaper, repeated so often they become part of the background noise. If that's the case, why invest so many resources into something that does not make a measurable difference?

The answer is cultural. It is what we do. Because of the copycat nature of our business, every station feels they must have some kind of line. As a large-market general manager once said to me, "It's that zing, that special thing at the end that makes a promo feel right."

The issue goes beyond ineffectiveness. By basing position/brand on a market void, then trying to fill that void with manufactured content, stations sometimes place barriers between themselves and the viewer. Consumers smell an inauthentic relationship a mile away.

Another Way of Thinking

During the 1990s, when I was running KARE 11 in Minneapolis, our station did not have a positioning line, though we had struggled mightily to come up with one.

It wasn't until after spending a week at a National Association of Broadcasters–sponsored seminar at Northwestern University's Media Management Center that I finally grasped the obvious: KARE 11 was the name of our brand. KARE 11 was our brand.

It wasn't that our station cared more about the community than journalistic leader WCCO or breaking news leader KSTP. We clearly did not. What we did have was a relationship with viewers, based in part on the personalities of our anchors, which viewers identified as KARE 11. This relationship was brought to mind when people saw our call letters. Fortunately for us, it was a strong and ingrained position that was based on enjoyment of watching our product, not the "big J" content the other stations were known for.

As a result of this understanding, news director Janet Mason and I believed we could broaden our brand by adding more in-depth journalism without compromising the things viewers enjoyed so much about the station. We would have to provide the heavier content in a manner that did not change our brand: interesting, great video, sometimes offbeat. Within two years, research was showing viewers saw KARE 11's journalism on the same level as WCCO but enjoyed it more. We eventually dominated every newscast in the market and enjoyed some of the highest demographic ratings in the country.

Defined by the Consumer

To truly understand brand as it applies to television, we need to not think of it as "advertising." Instead, we will use a business school definition: brand is determined by the consumer, not the business. A brand image is the result of the consumer's total interaction, both large and small, with a product. Brand is established over years. Like culture, brand is powerful and, once established, very difficult to change.

To better understand this, let's look at a nonbroadcast example: Hyundai cars.

When Hyundai entered the US market during the 1980s, it was with an inexpensive car that quickly developed a reputation for unreliability. It did not take long for Hyundai's brand to become established: "cheap Korean car that is unreliable." That was not the brand Hyundai wanted, but it was what the consumer believed; therefore, it was Hyundai's brand.

Hyundai's response was to concentrate on quality control and reliability, but the damage was done. Even though the product was now reliable, no amount of advertising could change the consumer's mind. Then Hyundai came up with a brilliant solution. They introduced the one hundred thousand–mile warranty. Over time, the Hyundai brand began to change until it became: "cheap Korean car that is reliable."

This was a better brand but, of course, still not the one Hyundai wanted. They wanted to sell a more expensive car, so they began to add options in the base price that other manufacturers charged for. Slowly their brand changed to: "has everything Japanese cars offer, but cheaper."

Hyundai then went for the kill. With a reputation for reliability and good value, they competed for the best US designers. Suddenly, Hyundai cars were fashionable. That eventually changed their brand to: "less expensive car I am not ashamed to drive."

Hyundai's brand did not morph overnight, nor did it completely lose the roots of its original brand, but by creating a much better product while retaining a lower price point, Hyundai developed a compelling brand.

The important thing about the Hyundai example is that in each stage, their brand changed because the reality of their product changed. Advertising supported that reality. Consumers create brands based on what they believe is real, not on hopes, dreams, or advertising.

One footnote to the Hyundai story. Hyundai's development of the Genesis line of high-end cars to compete with Lexus and

Mercedes-Benz created a brand conflict. "Less expensive car I am not ashamed to drive" is not a brand consumers associate with a $60,000 car. Eventually, Hyundai made a smart decision. They spun Genesis off as a separate franchise, just as Toyota did with Lexus and Nissan did with Infiniti. This allowed Genesis to develop its own brand.

Understanding the Consumer

Media strategist John Lavine says there are three things that define today's consumer:

• Overwhelming information. During the next hour, more information will be created than in any past hour in the history of the world. Making sense of all this has never been more difficult.

• Increasing complexity. Everything is getting more complex. Try to figure out the electronics in a new car. Try to understand the latest updates on your mobile operating system—good luck if your phone is iOS and your tablet is Android. While you are at it, choose which cell carrier to use. The list never ends.

• Twenty-four-hour fixed time limit. If you slept eight hours last night, you have 960 minutes left to get everything else done today.

Consumers, especially women who work outside the home and have children, have never felt more overwhelmed. I know. In seminars, I usually ask, "How many people in this room are tired? How many feel overwhelmed? How many wish their lives were simpler? How many would like to have a little more time to themselves?" Women are the first to raise their hands.

Why are these things important? Because we must understand how and why today's consumers make decisions. Not just media decisions but all decisions.

The Essential Nature of Brand

Because they are so busy, with so little time, consumers must have a way to shorthand the complex world they live in. Consumers do not navigate by brand because they want to. They do it because they have no other choice. Consumers don't actually think this out, nor would they necessarily use the term *brand*. Brand is simply what makes it possible to get through the complexities of the day. Like habit, brand does not necessarily function on a conscious level. Brand makes it possible to perform daily functions without having to constantly make choices.

Let's look at two nonmedia examples of successful brands:

Keurig Coffee Pods

Brand: quick, not messy, upscale. The Keurig brand is brilliant because it is not price sensitive. It is not even about coffee. Keurig's brand is about selling time back to consumers.

Keurig is also seen as an upscale product, which appeals to the aspirational desire we all experience to some degree. Sure, a consumer might shop for the least-expensive pods, but if the Keurig decision was based on price, we would still be brewing pots using bagged grounds and a $19.95 Mr. Coffee.

Do consumers actually stop and think about why they use a Keurig? Of course not. It all happens on a subconscious level, but it is nonetheless real.

Jimmy John's Subs

Like Keurig, Jimmy John's is also in the time business, only blatantly so. If you want a custom sub made your way, stand in line at Subway. If you want to save time, call Jimmy John's. Jimmy John's also makes the consumer's life easy by reducing the decision to a number. Just for fun, I sometimes ask groups which number Jimmy John's they like best. Many are able to tell me. Brand is the reason upscale shoppers might pick Costco over Sam's Club, or Target over Walmart. It's not about money. It's about brand value. Other shoppers might choose Sam's over Costco, or Walmart over Target, precisely because it is about the money. Saving money is the brand value. Either way, those decisions are driven by consumer perception of brand.

Brand Navigation

Every business or enterprise has a brand. Sometimes the brand is positive, sometimes it is negative, but it is always determined by the consumer and based on the consumer's experience.

Because today's consumers are so busy and have so little time, weak brands often do not achieve cognition. Even strong brands that are not relevant can fail to have an impact. To be effective, a brand must be relevant to a consumer's life.

One of the problems we have in media is that fragmentation has created far too many brands for any consumer to navigate. Consider how many brands of similar/same products (e.g., peanut butter, tea, or coffee) are available in a grocery store. Most are so weak they have no impact on potential users. Media is exactly the same way.

Brand is important to television stations because it defines the real connection, positive or negative, between us and our viewers. Understanding your brand creates a framework for decision-making, a light on the pathway to success.

Your real brand, as expressed by your most loyal viewers, is probably not an advertising line or a slogan. It is an expression of the reasons those viewers chose your product. It is the first thing that comes to mind when they see your logo, call letters, or channel position.

It is not unusual for successful stations to have the brand "That's who I've always watched" or "I like their people." Last-place stations might be "I don't think they are very good" or "That's the station that keeps changing."

The irony of brand in our industry is that, like Hyundai, we have the ability to modify our brands in ways that will increase viewer usage of our products. That requires having the courage to understand ourselves and consumers through the consumers' eyes, then doing the hard work of real brand building.

A station whose brand is "That's who I've always watched" is actually in a precarious position even though they are the market leader. The temptation is to change nothing until they are in trouble. The better way is to use their current strength to build something even stronger.

Defining Your Real Brand

It would be nice if we could sit down with our management team and define our brand. Unfortunately, that is not possible. We are simply too close to the product, too invested to see ourselves through the eyes of the consumers. The only way to actually define our real brand is through the consumers.

One method is to start with the proprietary attitude-and-opinion surveys about local news most stations already do. These studies are not designed specifically to understand brand, but they do measure a number of components of brand and provide an overall sense of consumer attitudes toward a station.

Another way is through focus groups led by independent experts who know how to probe deeply. The downside of focus groups is they can be hijacked by one or two vocal proponents.

Some researchers have had success with individual interviews of consumers, but this method is also time consuming and can be expensive.

Whatever method you use, keep in mind that viewers do not think of television the same way we do. We like to verbalize all the nuances that separate stations. The consumer doesn't do any of that. She simply knows what she likes and what she doesn't because once a brand has been established in her mind, there is no reason to revisit the subject. It is only when you probe that she will actually think about and verbalize a station's brand.

Because television does not exist in a vacuum, you need to also understand your competitors' brands. At some point, you are going to create a strategic plan to modify your brand. When that happens, it will be important to not try to duplicate another station's established brand. Let's say your primary competitor is known for their extreme community service efforts. If that's the case, do not go in that direction. They own that brand. Acknowledge they own it and go your own way.

Summary

Whether they be called positions or brands, slogans have always been used by television stations to describe their news. Some, such as "Where the News Comes First" at KCRA, have been effective because they represented genuine viewer benefits the consumer saw on the air. Others have not been effective because they represented advertising claims rather than unique viewer benefits.

The copycat nature of television means virtually every station in a market uses their brand lines the same ways: in graphics, at the end of stories, and at the end of promotional announcements. This sameness in use and the lack of product distinctness connected to the brand statement mean most produce little effect on viewer behavior.

Audience fragmentation and lack of viewer time make it imperative for stations to understand their true brands. This can only be done through the eyes of viewers.

Effective brands can be a genuine advantage for a television station only when it provides unique viewer benefits that the consumers recognize as being important to their lives.

Brands are always built on reality. Understanding a station's current brand is the beginning point of creating a genuinely effective brand.

Key Takeaways

- Most television "brands" are ineffective because they are primarily advertising lines, not descriptions of unique viewer benefits.
- Consumers, not stations, define brands.
- Building an effective brand begins with understanding a station's true current brand.

5

STRATEGIC PLANNING

If you have reached a department head level in television, you have likely been through a strategic planning process. Different companies have various takes on the mechanisms of long-term planning, but all share the same core idea of creating a framework that will result in achieving specific station financial goals.

Individual stations are unique, so no two plans are exactly alike, but all share the idea that a strong plan will serve as both a guide and measurement of success. Most begin with some kind of overall statement of what the station hopes to achieve over the next year, or multiple years, followed by specific goals and metrics to measure achievement. It is not unusual for a plan to have subgoals down to the department level. Some companies believe in complex plans that are highly detailed, while others prefer broad strokes.

When I ran stations for Gannett (now Tegna), our strategic planning process was laborious and sometimes painful. The final work required a large loose-leaf binder. The process was so complex that we followed a checklist to make sure we didn't miss anything.

If you've been involved with this kind of planning, you know that Helmuth von Moltke was right when he said, "No battle plan survives contact with the enemy."

The more complex and detailed a plan is, the more likely it will become not just a casualty but a doorstop not looked at until the next strategic planning process. You can actually predict this based on the management team's attitude when the plan is first completed. If everyone involved gives a sigh of relief, odds are the plan will be put away, gathering dust until the following year. That was certainly the case for out team. It was with bated breath we submitted our plan to corporate each year, hoping it would be accepted without major changes.

The more complex a plan is, the more goals and subgoals it contains, the more likely it will be seen by staff as not relevant to their daily activities. Complex plans are particularly vulnerable when a competitor changes the rules.

This is not to suggest the strategic planning process is unimportant. A strong plan, understood and believed in by both management and staff, always undergirds success. Think of it as the big picture, a definition of who you are and what you believe in as an organization. It is a way to keep everyone on the same page and thus working to achieve the same goals.

The question then is how to create a strategic plan that is actually useful.

If your company has a specific planning process, then by all means follow it and do so with enthusiasm. However, if the plan is to be actually used, its goals must be realistic, achievable, and, above all, believed in by your staff, so don't be afraid to look at the process differently.

Three Views

In order to better understand strategic planning, let's look at it three ways. First will be a traditional process many stations follow. Second will be some alternate thinking that might help streamline the process. Finally, we will look at an actual case study of a television station that had a failed plan followed by a successful plan later.

The Traditional Process

When television stations talk about strategy, they are normally talking about finding some particular viewer benefit they can emphasize in their newscasts and marketing.

The process often starts with a major news study comparing your station with others in the market. Talent comparisons are an important component, but one has to remember that talent rankings are affected by station strength. In other words, anchors on number-one stations will normally be ranked higher than talent on number-three stations. That's simply a function of viewing patterns.

Anchors can be a powerful reason for viewers to choose a particular station, but for the most part, the overall success of a station also drives anchor popularity. Ideally, the two work hand in hand.

The heart of research is a look at newscast elements ranked by viewer interest. Viewers are asked to compare a long list of news content elements by importance—topics such as weather, breaking news, in-depth coverage, community coverage, investigations, lifestyle, and so on. Once the list is ranked, viewers are then asked which stations best provide those elements.

The idea is to determine voids in the market. For instance, let's say "holding city hall accountable" ranks high on the list, but no station is given credit for strong reporting on city hall. A last-place station might decide to beef up city hall reporting, using it as a marketing tool to attract viewers.

In practice, the top-rated coverage elements, such as weather and breaking news, already belong to strong stations. Investigative reporting, which is hard to do well, is often seen as a void. A last-place station might decide to "own" investigations. Reporters are reassigned, resources are reallocated, and a marketing plan claiming WXXX is "the investigative station" is launched to high hopes and great expectation. Like the branding/positioning lines we discussed earlier, this approach can have merit, but in practice, it rarely makes a major difference. It seems like a good idea, is based on research, and fills a void in the market. Why wouldn't it increase ratings?

The problem with basing strategy on voids in the market is that viewers rarely choose a favorite television station because of specialized reporting. There are, of course, instances where this approach has worked, but for the most part, it is hard to document success. Remember also, as we learned in the branding chapter, a brand is created by every contact a station has with a viewer, not just the things the station wants to emphasize.

Now that voids have been established, it's time to come up with the catchy phrase, that thing every reporter says at the end of his or her story, that every promo reinforces at the end of the spot.

I once asked a news director why he labeled everything "Accuracy Matters." His answer—and I'm not making this up—was, "We asked the viewers through research if accuracy mattered, and they said yes."

At the end of the day, like Hyundai, you must begin with reality, then adjust your product based on what the consumer wants, not what sounds good or seems to have worked at other stations.

The real issue is that entrenched last-place stations constantly look for magic bullets that will catapult news ratings to first place. The reality is that the viewer-decision process is much more complex. It is based on long-term brand perceptions. Under the best of circumstances, changing viewer behavior is a long-term process. That's why one of the favorite phrases in our industry is, "It takes a lot of time to turn an aircraft carrier."

The Message Dilution Problem

Another problem with basing strategy on market voids is that stations tend to add the new and greatest idea to existing priorities, never taking anything away. The last station I was involved with turning around had twelve different names and program elements on the air, many with their own graphic look and feel. Every time the station came up with a new and better idea, it was added to the mix without taking anything away. Research showed viewers had forgotten the station's name.

When thinking about strategy, what you eliminate is as important as what you add.

None of this is to demean research, which is critical to understanding your audience. But research should not be looked at in a vacuum. Stations need to use every tool in their arsenal to support building an effective brand.

In today's consumer-driven, multiplatform world, where decisions are based on brand, it is critical for stations to have an overall station strategy, not just a news strategy.

The biggest problem with the traditional way of forming a strategy is that it does not look at the station's relationship with the viewer as a whole.

A Different Way of Thinking

Let me be clear that there is no single right or wrong way to create an effective strategy. Let's now look at a different way, but certainly not the only way, to think about strategic planning.

Rather than beginning by looking at voids in the market, I've found it can be more productive to first take a holistic view of the market, understanding the uniqueness of the community and what makes the area tick, and a sociological view of the area, then review the television landscape, including each station's strengths and weaknesses from a viewer perspective. This can be hard to do without outside help, so a skilled facilitator can sometimes be helpful. Think of it as a kind of SWAT but a deeper dig.

Instead of beginning with what you want the outcome to be, begin with understanding who you actually are, the reality of your situation. Every station wants to be number one, but does your staff really believe that is possible? Do you work for a company that will fully support that goal? How do you feel about risk? Do you have the guts for cultural change? Are you willing to remove things the station has done for years? Are you prepared to lose some viewers in order to attract a particular viewer profile? These are hard questions that require honest answers. In fact, you need to ask yourself these questions long before beginning the planning process. Strategies based on hopes and dreams waste time and resources better used elsewhere.

When I was managing KARE 11, I hired an outsider named Dr. Bob Terry to lead our management group through a strategic process. During the course of the first day, our people talked about our creativity, our willingness to create change, and our desire to go our own way. After listening to hours of this, Terry said something profound: "You people have put together a nice list of things you would like to believe about yourselves, but when I listen, that's not what I really hear. I hear, 'Beat WCCO.' That's who you really are."

That statement from Terry made us realize that our concentration on WCCO was causing us to let our main competitor set our agenda. We needed a radical change of mind so that we could go our own way. As long as another station was the standard, we would always be at their mercy.

It sounds strange to begin with a market and station analysis as opposed to viewer research, but it is important because at the end of the day, you must create a plan the station's staff will actually believe in. That is much easier to do when you start with reality.

Role of the General Manager

Because news is the heart of any station's strategy, it seems natural that the news director leads the process. I think a better way is for the general manager to be the leader. News may be the most important part, but a station's brand is first and foremost the responsibility of the general manager.

This is not to minimize the role of the news director. The news director is a key player and the critical product implementer. As we will discuss in the news chapter, the nature of a news director's job makes looking down the road difficult. Turning station planning over to the news director—or any other department head, for that matter—can limit the vision of the station. Like it or not, the general manager must set the station agenda.

Consultants might be able to help, but a strategy lifted from another station does not take into account the individuality of your station and market.

Back in my consulting days, time after time, we would design a station's strategy and seemingly get buy-in from all the players, only to get lip service when it came to implementation. Just because the news director does not take the lead in planning, that does not mean a successful strategy can be implemented without full buy-in from the news director.

Station Position Affects Strategy

My first general manager's job was at WFMY, the CBS affiliate in Greensboro, North Carolina. WFMY in those days was a legendary station. Just prior to my arrival, they had achieved the highest ratings in station history. My job, according to my boss, was "don't mess it up." It was the hardest job I ever had.

Because I was new, I fell into the trap of playing defense, trying to protect everything the station had achieved in the past. During my four years, the station somehow stayed on top, but that was because I got out in time. I would have been far better advised to create a strategic plan that took the station into the future. If I had the same job today, I would forget competitors and build on the station's powerful base.

Time after time, dominant stations have lost their power because they did not have a strategic plan for the future. Part of the problem is the inverse relationship between profit and risk. The more profitable a station, the less anyone is willing to take the risk of doing something different. The other problem, frankly, is the sense of superiority that often comes with being a leading station.

If you are running a dominant station, it is especially important to begin the strategic planning process by understanding why your ratings are so strong. Somehow over the years, you have built a strong relationship with viewers. What is the core of that relationship? How can you extend it to younger viewers?

The Turnaround

After the WFMY experience, I decided to spend the rest of my career doing turnarounds.

Turnarounds are not for everyone. You have to enjoy what seems to others an insurmountable challenge, be focused enough to not abandon the strategy when you make a tactical mistake, yet still be willing to listen to department heads when they say you are wrong.

A certain level of stress is part of your job no matter what, but stress can be a much bigger issue when doing a turnaround. If stress is a problem for you, consider getting some professional help. Learning to compartmentalize is essential to your well-being. If you can't do that, you will stay awake at night.

After working my way up to running stations in Minneapolis and then Chicago, when Viacom bought CBS and many of us cashed out, my wife reminded me I had promised her we would someday move back to North Carolina. Ironically, Hearst had just bought the NBC affiliate in that same market we had lived in before, so I ended up back in the same town I began my GM career, only this time at the last-place NBC affiliate.

In addition to running the station, Hearst also allowed me to work for Northwestern University's Media Management Center. The combination of an underperforming TV station, access to some of the best minds at the Kellogg School of Management, and Hearst's deep commitment to their stations meant we could try things at WXII in a different way from anything in the past.

In order to understand the full challenge we faced, here is the actual case study later taught at Northwestern:

WXII Case Study

This case represents the Greensboro / Winston-Salem / High Point Television Market in the year 2000.

Background

Three medium-sized North Carolina cities—Greensboro, Winston-Salem, and High Point—make up the forty-seventh largest television market in the United States.

Located in the upper-central part of the state, each of the cities is distinctive. Greensboro, the largest community (population 223,000), is an economic leader and the city best known outside North Carolina. Greensboro is home to the regional airport, often hosts ACC basketball championships, and boasts one of the nation's oldest PGA tournaments. The local newspaper, the Greensboro News & Record, is the largest daily paper in the region.

Greensboro is located in Guilford County, as is the smaller city of High Point just a short drive south.

A more blue-collar area than Greensboro, High Point (population 86,000) hosts the twice-yearly international furniture market. When thinking of High Point, residents and nonresidents alike usually think of furniture. While High Point shares the same county school system as Greensboro, in all other ways, it is a distinctive community. *The High Point Enterprise*, a daily paper, competes with a regionalized edition of the *News & Record*.

Just to the west of Guilford County is Forsyth County, home of Winston-Salem (population 186,000). Approximately thirty-five miles to the west of Greensboro, the Winston-Salem community has an unspoken but long-standing rivalry with the larger city.

Known primarily as the home of R. J. Reynolds Tobacco, Winston-Salem was at one time also a banking and textile center. In recent years, the city has struggled to diversify and lose its reputation as part of the "old South." Even so, economic growth has continued to lag behind Greensboro. Wake Forest University, located within the city limits, has taken a leadership role in this area, using its medical school to create a biotech center in the heart of downtown Winston-Salem. The local daily paper is the *Winston-Salem Journal*.

In general, the Greensboro / Winston-Salem / High Point market has lagged in both population growth and economic development behind neighbors Charlotte and Raleigh. However, the region has reason to believe growth will come in the future. Relatively low land cost, a moderate climate, beautiful topography, access to several interstate highways, a strong community college system, and a transitioning workforce should make the area attractive to companies looking to relocate to the Sun Belt. In addition, the region has outstanding medical care, something important to retirees looking to move south.

Prior to the 1960s, Greensboro, Winston-Salem, and High Point were separate television markets. The three communities eventually merged into one market (population 1,124,000), yet the cities continued to maintain quite separate identities. While the region is known by many as "the Piedmont Triad," efforts to convince the cities to work together have met with little success. Rivalry is common.

Television Stations

The oldest station in the region is WFMY, the CBS affiliate. WFMY is a longtime ratings leader and the only station located in Greensboro. Solid news coverage, community involvement, and a history of being one of the highest-rated CBS affiliates in the country have caused many Greensboro residents to think of WFMY as "my television station."

Though still highly rated, in recent years, WFMY has experienced some erosion of younger viewers to another station, WGHP.

Located in High Point, WGHP was for many years an ABC affiliate. During the 1990s, WGHP was purchased by Fox and affiliation switched (the ABC affiliation went to WXLV, a weak UHF station with a minor news operation and little viewership).

Because WGHP is located in the smallest of the three cities, smart management in the 1980s created a "regional" identity that deemphasized the High Point location. The addition of Fox also allowed WGHP to produce a 10:00 p.m. newscast that did not compete with the other stations' 11:00 p.m. broadcasts. WGHP purposefully created a sharper, "more hip" look and feel designed to appeal to younger viewers.

Far more personality oriented than WFMY, WGHP's regional strategy has worked. By attracting viewers from High Point, Greensboro, and Winston-Salem, WGHP has been able to gather a large group of younger viewers, surpassing WFMY. WGHP viewers are also quite loyal, seeing the station as more energetic and interesting to watch. Many WGHP viewers cite "personalities" as a primary reason they prefer WGHP's newscasts.

Like the other two communities, Winston-Salem has its "own" television station. WXII is an NBC affiliate with a history of good ratings within Winston-Salem but little viewing in Guilford and other counties to the east. Unfortunately for WXII, the station's news ratings have always lagged far behind both WFMY and WGHP. Part of WXII's problem is geographic. It is seen in the more populous eastern region as "the Winston-Salem station." WXII has also traditionally spent less on its news operation than the other stations. Viewers have noticed, and many see WXII's news product as inferior. As a result of all these factors, WXII has only been able to achieve an 8 percent preference level in Guilford, the region's largest county. This lack of viewing in Greensboro and High Point means most of WXII's newscasts are rated number three.

Not only are WXII's newscast ratings lower than the other stations, but syndicated programming is also inferior. WXII managers pride themselves on spending less for programming than other area stations. As one station executive said, "We may have lower ratings, but we also have lower expenses, meaning we make more money."

During the mid-1990s, executives at WXII found themselves faced not only with a small audience in the east but a shrinking audience in the west. WGHP's efforts at regionalization were being felt by WXII.

WXII's response was both bold and risky. Station management decided to admit defeat in the east while concentrating all resources to rebuild audience in the west. News coverage, sales efforts, and community involvement in Guilford County were terminated. A news bureau in Greensboro was closed and WXII's phone number removed from the directory. Viewers who called the station with story ideas about Guilford County were told by the assignment desk, "We don't cover Greensboro."

As resources were moved to the west, WXII created a new station slogan: "Complete Local Coverage of the Western Piedmont."

Among other things, a full-time news crew was assigned to find stories in counties west and northwest of Winston-Salem. The station began to attend community events in western counties. Even weather coverage was changed. When standing in front of weather maps, WXII meteorologists stood over Greensboro, covering that city and High Point. Forecasts, temperatures, and other information only applied to Winston-Salem and areas to the west and northwest. A massive on-air campaign was also created to promote the station's new slogan.

Interestingly, as NBC prime time did well during the mid-1990s, so did WXII's strategy of only covering part of the market. In one May rating book, WXII actually tied for first place in late news demographics. This success encouraged management, and efforts to place all resources in only one part of the market were redoubled.

Unfortunately, WXII's strategy of hypercovering one part of the market had a number of weaknesses. First, cutting off the fastest-growing part of the market restricted WXII's long-term ratings and revenue growth. Second, WGHP countered the threat by increasing its own coverage of the west while still maintaining a geographically neutral on-air stance. Because many viewers perceived WGHP's product and talent to be more sophisticated than WXII's, many upscale viewers were lured away. WGHP also created a news-sharing partnership with the *Winston-Salem Journal*.

WFMY did not react to WXII's strategy. WFMY continued to cover the entire market with an emphasis on Greensboro. Moreover, WFMY's early news lead-in, *The Oprah Winfrey* Show, allowed the station to attract news viewers from all parts of the market.

In 1999, WXII was purchased by a large television station company. News-centric, the new company had a stated goal of being the news leader in every market. After reviewing station strategy, company executives announced they were uncomfortable with the "Complete Local Coverage of the Western Piedmont" concept. They felt strongly that a station could only become a true number-one player if it covered the entire market. Station executives defended the "Western Piedmont" strategy, pointing out that ratings were the highest ever achieved by the station. Moreover, retreat from such a public position could bring on disaster.

WXII managers also pointed out that station facilities, equipment, pay scales, staffing levels, and syndicated programming were inadequate when compared to WFMY and WGHP. Company officials countered with a promise to make significant investment in all areas of the station. However, investment must also bring return. While company executives preferred to not dictate local strategy, they strongly felt reasonable long-term return was unlikely without full market coverage.

With great reluctance, station officials withdrew from the "Western Piedmont" concept and returned to full-market coverage. The new slogan was simply "Complete Local Coverage."

As predicted, ratings began to decline. Viewers in the west recognized that WXII was no longer exclusively covering their area. Some switched their loyalty from WXII to WGHP. Viewers in the east continued watching WFMY or WGHP.

In 2000, WXII's longtime general manager announced his retirement, and a new general manager was recruited and given the assignment of making whatever changes necessary to move WXII from last to first place.

Upon arrival, the new general manager found work already under way to modernize the technical plant. Money for a new newsroom had also been allocated, but planning for the facility had not yet begun.

Unfortunately, with ratings dropping and no clear sense of direction, staff and middle management were demoralized. Their one opportunity to win something, anything, had been taken away with cancellation of the "Western Piedmont" strategy. They also thought the new direction had injured their relationship with core viewers.

Moreover, the staff felt they only did two things well enough to be competitive with other stations. The first was weather. Because weather patterns usually move west to east and the station owned a sophisticated Doppler radar, WXII often showed a small ratings increase during severe weather. The second was in-depth coverage of big stories. Though not reflected in the ratings, the news staff felt they sometimes produced stories that had more depth.

After being introduced to the staff at a station-wide meeting, the new general manager said, "We are going to put together a strategy that will make WXII number one. I don't know yet what the strategy will be, but I do know we will achieve our goal. Within the next five years, WXII will become number one." There was no response from the audience. Finally, one person raised her hand to ask a question: "Why are you really here?"

If you are familiar with the case study process, you know they never tell you how things actually came out. The idea is to make the students analyze options and make their own decisions as to the best course of action. In using this study at the Media Management Center, students invariably recommended WXII return to its previous position of "Complete Local Coverage of the Western Piedmont." They simply thought going for first place was a hill too far.

In reality, at the end of five years, WXII was in a three-way tie with WFMY and WGHP. At the end of ten years, WXII was in first place, WGHP was second, and WFMY was third. In one decade, WXII and WFMY reversed positions. How did this happen?

The station used a five-step process that worked like this:

Step One: Operational Excellence

> **You first have to learn the rules**
> **in order to break them properly.**
> **—Unknown**

There is no magic formula, plan, or great idea that will instantly transform a last-place station into a first-place station, but without a foundation of operational excellence, nothing else is possible. Operational excellence is the cost of admission.

Operational excellence includes everything that makes a product great. The right content, appealing anchors, graphics, set, lead-in programming, all the things that cause one station to look and feel better than the rest.

Unfortunately, those of us in television often confuse operational excellence with strategy, thinking that by creating a better product, we will beat the number-one station. This never works. Never really has worked. There are dozens, if not hundreds, of failed news directors and general managers who staked their careers on winning by simply doing a better job. Why does this approach not work? Because consumers will not abandon their favorite brand for a similar brand they have no relationship with, even if the new brand is somewhat better.

There is one exception to this rule. If a favorite brand materially disappoints loyal consumers—and I mean materially, such as failing to cover a major story—then viewers will start to consider other choices. The earliest example I can think of came back in 1972, when WDSU in New Orleans, one of America's then-great television stations, was sold to corporate owners who cut costs to the point that many of the station's longtime personalities left and the quality of the product deteriorated. This became a public embarrassment. Viewers were so offended they changed to

WWL, a station that had always been in second place. WWL then held on to first place for almost forty-five years. WDSU's current owners are doing a good job of bringing the station back, but they've had to overcome mistakes others made decades ago.

This is not to suggest operational excellence is not important. It is the critical first step toward first place, but it is not a strategy, nor is it enough to make a station win.

In WXII's case, the station was in terrible shape, so the list of operational items was long: anchors, quality of staff, equipment, facilities, sets, and graphics, just to name a few.

Step Two: Belief

Whether you believe you can do a thing or not, you are right.
—Henry Ford

As you saw in the case study, WXII had never been a leader, so there was no basis for staff to believe that things could actually get better, much less make the station a winner.

Belief cannot be instilled by promises or pep talks. It must be demonstrated. In WXII's case, that meant doing such a good job over a long period of time that the staff began to believe they might actually be able to win—at least on some dimension.

Over time, WXII's newscasts began to do two things better than the other stations. The first was coverage of big stories. This paid off one Thursday night when a beloved local radio personality named Big Paul was killed in a motorcycle accident just outside of High Point.

During the 11:00 p.m. news that night, both WFMY and WGHP led with the Big Paul story, devoting about five minutes' worth of content before going on to other stories.

WXII did something completely different. Their entire late newscast, except for brief weather at the end, was devoted to coverage of Big Paul's death. Multiple reporters in multiple live locations did stories on every aspect of what was seen as a major loss to the community. Big Paul's coworkers gave emotional interviews, physicians at the hospital talked about the tragedy, police officers weighed in, other members of the motorcycle rally made comments, and on and on.

Because the story was so big, once WFMY and WGHP left the story, viewers started searching for more coverage. They found it at WXII. The next day's overnights showed that for the first time in station history, WXII resoundingly won a late newscast.

The Big Paul story did not change viewing habits, but it did give WXII's staff the confidence to believe in their ability to do something better than the other stations.

The second thing WXII did better was emergency weather. Because WXII owned the only live television radar, they already got some credit for emergency weather. This was expanded by upgrading staff and equipment, then extending coverage during severe weather. Because WXII was now owned by a news-centric company, they were able to interrupt any program for emergency weather, then stay on the air as long as necessary.

Extended coverage of big stories and coverage of emergency weather gave WXII two toeholds to believe in.

Step Three: Strategy

The essence of strategy is choosing what not to do.
—Michael Porter

I realize how unconventional it seems to just now be getting to strategy, but there is a reason. For a strategy to actually work, it must do three things. First, it must offer a genuine viewer benefit that is important enough to change viewer behavior. Second, it must be based on reality, not hope or voids in the market. Finally, a station's staff must believe in it. It is only after these three things are in place that implementing a strategy makes sense.

As WXII's staff began to believe in themselves, a bit of swagger started to appear. For the first time ever, people were enjoying coming to work. From all this came WXII's strategy. It was three statements on one piece of paper:

Win the Big Story

Win Weather

Have Some Fun

No loose-leaf binders, no subgoals, just constant encouragement that no matter what else happened, WXII would always do these three things. These were real things the staff actually believed in, so there was no need to explain their meaning. Just a constant reminder: "We own these things. We will never allow anyone to beat us in these three areas."

Notice there is nothing about ratings in the strategic statement. The staff could not control ratings, but they could control the three things in the strategic plan. Ratings would come later. Stan Leonard was right when he said, "First we will be best, then we will be first."

One reason television stations' strategies rarely work is because stations try to do too much. The strategy is added on top of everything else. That means the strategy eventually gets lost in the clutter or, and this is more common, becomes just a statement that does not mean anything.

In WXII's case, anything that did not advance the strategy hurt the strategy. That meant some activities that used up resources needed to be eliminated. Sacred cows, such as franchises, a dedicated consumer reporter, a health reporter, entertainment and lifestyle reports, even sports when not part of a big story, were rethought.

Of course, the station still produced balanced newscasts, but more emphasis was put on actual news coverage as opposed to features and other ancillary products.

> **Believe in something larger than yourself...**
> **get involved in some of the big ideas of our time.**
> —Barbara Bush

Once operational excellence is in place and you have a strategy your staff believes in, you now need a way to break through the clutter and put your station front and center with viewers. You need big ideas.

One Thursday afternoon, Bruce Wheeler, a local radio GM, and I were sitting in Reagan National Airport when an announcement was made over the public-address system that a group of World War II veterans was about to arrive on a chartered US Airways flight from somewhere in the Midwest. They were part of an organization called Honor Flight that was making sure veterans were able to visit the new World War II memorial in Washington, DC.

A band, police escorts, and spontaneous applause from virtually everyone in the terminal met the veterans. It was an emotional moment.

Bruce and I looked at each other and had the same idea—sending veterans from our part of North Carolina to Washington, DC.

As a result, WXII made a public commitment to send every World War II veteran in the station's viewing area to visit the World War II memorial at no charge. Working with area Rotary Clubs, the station raised more than $650,000 in donations, ranging from people writing checks to kids selling lemonade. It was a true community effort.

Each time a Flight of Honor charter left Piedmont Triad International Airport, WXII carried the event live. Each time a group returned, WXII carried that event live. Hundreds of people showed up for these events, cheering, waving American flags, and creating an incredible experience for the veterans. The very first flight included a Bataan Death March survivor, a member of the 101st Airborne who was part of the famous picture with Eisenhower the night before D-Day. Most were ordinary veterans who had simply done their duty. Some had never been on an airplane before. There were also two women: a nurse and actress Betty Lynn, who had played Thelma Lou on *The Andy Griffith Show*. Betty had been a sixteen-year-old USO performer in the South Pacific.

Flight of Honor struck an incredible emotional nerve in the community. The children, grandchildren, and great-grandchildren of these veterans were especially touched, but we were all moved. In the end, every veteran who wanted to go was sent.

WXII did the Flight of Honor campaign because it was the right thing to do. But the station gained because the campaign also gave viewers a connection with the station that no amount of marketing or advertising could ever have achieved. It worked because it was real.

Not the Only Way

The four-step process I've outlined is one way to approach strategy, but certainly not the only.

Whatever approach you decide to take, here are some elements worth keeping in mind:

1. Make sure your plan is based on realistic goals. Goals only have value if they are achievable.

2. Simplify the plan. Complexity is the enemy of achievement.

3. Choose a strategy that takes hard work. Strategies that are easy to achieve are also easy to copy. Don't be vulnerable to another station taking credit for your strategy.

4. Decide what you are willing to give up. You can't do every-

thing, so don't try.

Viewer Targeting

Because television is the last form of mass media, we forget that when it comes to our brand and strategy, our product cannot be all things to all people. Therefore, we need a target.

Because the bulk of our revenue is tied to advertising, we, of course, want to have sellable viewers, but overly broad advertising demographics complicates this. Adults ages twenty-five through fifty-four or women ages eighteen through forty-nine are not targets. They are results.

There are a number of ways to look at a target. Some stations think of their target as a person, perhaps a woman in her midthirties who is married, has children, and works outside the home.

Others look at psychographic targets—people who think alike and have common interests. Cohort groups are also popular.

Whatever method you choose, a target is a device that helps keep your product consistent.

It is important that you also think beyond stereotypes. Too many stations have gotten off track by offering things like health features and cooking they think will appeal to women. The reality is that working women go to television for news and weather, not features. Tablets and phones are much better sources of specialized content. For instance, I'm an avid woodworker, but that's not what I watch television news for.

The best way to learn about a target is to find out how she lives her life and how your ability to produce local news and information can aid her life.

Remember too that when you are successful with a target, you are also successful with those around your target, meaning the results you achieve will be much broader.

Summary

The goal of a strategic plan is to give a station a path to achieving specific goals that eventually lead to bottom-line financial results.

Some companies require stations to develop complex plans that are lengthy and difficult to achieve, making them less likely to be followed. A plan that goes on a shelf is of no value.

Plans should be as simple as possible. They must also achieve staff buy-in.

Because we live in a consumer-driven, brand-based world, research is a valuable tool in developing a strategic plan. However, simply finding market voids is too simplistic a way to use research.

Targeting is a key element of both branding and strategic planning.

Whatever planning process you follow, make sure it is clear, achievable, and has staff buy-in.

Key Takeaways

- **Make sure your plan is simple enough to actually be implemented.**
- **Research is important, but it is only one element of planning.**
- **There is no one right or wrong way to create a strategic plan.**
- **Narrow your focus. You cannot be all things to all people.**
- **Employee belief is critical.**

6

Leading Management Teams

As we have discussed, one central attribute of every great leader is the ability to inspire others to achieve a common goal, not as robots simply executing the leader's plan but as thinkers in their own right who add their own experience, skills, and thoughts to the daily effort. This is especially true when it comes to department heads.

Empowering these department leaders to make important decisions can supercharge results because it takes advantage of their own unique backgrounds and experience. The ability to trust department heads, even though they will occasionally make mistakes, is one mark of a confident leader.

As the person ultimately responsible for success of the brand, you must also know which decisions require your input and which do not. For instance, I would never suggest which stories a news director should select for coverage or how a sales manager should price a buy. But I would always want to be involved in news philosophy, talent hiring, and other big-picture news decisions. I would also want to sign off on a sales manager's pricing philosophy.

Because part of your role is that of coach, you want to spend enough time with each department head to understand departmental issues and to either be a sounding board or offer guidance where appropriate. Sometimes there is a fine line between giving guidance and micromanagement because not all decisions are clear-cut. There are also some decisions of such great importance only the general manager should make them.

The downside of having strong department heads is at some point they will come into conflict with each other. This is guaranteed to happen. Managing conflict in a way that leads to mutual respect and positive results is one of the greatest challenges every general manager faces.

Department Heads

The department head team is quite small, usually six or seven people—normally, a general sales manager, news director, creative services director, chief engineer, programming head, and business manager. Some stations may be organized slightly differently, but whatever titles they hold, these are your key managers. They are often strong personalities, so some will always be competitive with each other. Your job is to mold them into a team, working together to achieve common station goals.

Left to their own devices, the default position of departments is to form silos, each seeking to achieve their own goals without regard to other needs in the station. Preventing silos, or breaking them up when they occur, is a big part of your daily job.

Some general managers believe in retreats and team-building exercises, others choose to act as arbiter between departments, and some choose to live with the silos. There is no clear right or wrong way to build a team, but know this: unless your department head group is aligned and able to work together, you will never achieve big goals.

Molding a group of people who are leaders in their own right begins with understanding what drives them. These are people who have worked their way up to department heads, so they are driven to achieve personal success. Motivating them to work as a team starts with helping them understand that group success is the best way to advance their own careers. This is one reason why an effective general manager must be able to articulate a vision people are willing to believe in.

Of course, there are always the outliers, people who have reached a certain point in their careers and for whatever reason are not interested in moving further up the line. Some may be tied to the area. Others might have fulfilled their ambition. Whatever the reason, you must take the time to also understand what makes these people tick. There is nothing wrong with the person who, for family or other reasons, wants to stay in the area or simply does not want to advance his or her career. If not advancement, what is it he or she does want? Pride of being part of the best station? A sense of professionalism? Some other positive attribute? Know what those drivers are so that you can help fulfill them.

Occasionally, you will run into a department head who simply wants the power of a silo. I once had to let a chief engineer go because he could not understand achieving overall station goals was more important than running his department in an arbitrary manner.

Run stations long enough and you occasionally have to part ways with a department head. I've always felt like doing this was a failure on my part, but nonetheless, I had to do it. Everyone must be on the same team.

Looking back over my career, the most successful stations I ran always generated new general managers from the department head ranks, in some cases six or seven. Group success always breeds individual success.

Information Is Power

A second driver is information. I've made it a practice to share as much information as possible with the department head group. Trusting them to keep the information confidential gives them a sense the group is special—which it is. For instance, I often invite the entire department head group to research presentations. In theory, only the news director and creative services director need to see the station's confidential research, but trusting the information with other key managers helps build the team. Plus, you never know what a general sales manager or chief engineer might add to the discussion.

When surveys ask employees what is important to them, information is always high on the list. Everyone wants to be on the inside. Knowing things that are only discussed among the team brings the team together in a way that makes them feel special.

Shared Goals

A third way to mold the group into a team is to create situations where they have to work together to achieve a common goal. Let's say the network decides to reformat morning news cut-ins. Asking the news director and general sales manager to come up with a plan for dividing inventory forces them to work together to achieve the best outcome.

More than anything else, simply making sure there is constant interaction between department heads pays off. For years, I resisted holding a daily operations meeting because I felt my constant interaction with each department head, combined with our weekly meeting, did the same thing. Once I finally tried the daily meetings, I realized how wrong I had been. Even fifteen minutes together each morning brings out a lot of information everyone needs to know. It also solves a lot of problems.

Esprit de Corps

Finally, there is an esprit de corps that comes from being part of a high-performance team, a special feeling that only comes with joint success. The greater esprit de corps is developed, the easier it will be for department heads to make decisions that advance the station agenda. When a sales manager is willing to give up inventory to raise news ratings, it is because the sales manager is able to see the long-term benefits. Likewise, when a news director is willing to accept more inventory in newscasts than normal for a limited period of time, such as during elections, it is because the news director realizes that supporting the sales manager's needs is an investment worth making.

Key Managers

Although titles and responsibilities vary between stations, every operation has key non–department head managers who make the place work. If department heads are captains, these folks are the sergeants.

Examples would be assistant news directors; executive producers; local, national, and digital sales managers; assistant chief engineers; master control supervisors—you get the picture.

Key managers are not only critical to the operation; from their ranks come the next department heads and, in some cases, general managers. Therefore, part of a general manager's job is to make sure these people are developing skills that will benefit their current work and prepare them for the future.

Key managers are not privy to the same kind of confidential information as department heads, but keeping them in the loop as appropriate is a sign that you value their contributions to the organization. Group e-mails about industry news is one way to achieve this.

Every station has a department head e-mail grouping. Adding a management team grouping that includes both department heads and key managers is one way to recognize their importance.

Another way to encourage key managers is for department heads to send congratulatory e-mails when big achievements happen. Copying the general manager on the e-mail allows you to add your congratulations and, where appropriate, forward to someone in corporate. This expands the group of people recognizing the achievement, especially when the corporate person then sends a congratulatory note. This kind of recognition is a powerful motivator and a tool every manager should have in their arsenal.

The Danger of Silos

However you choose to organize your station's managers, remember that your most important management job is to make sure everyone is on the same team, seeking to achieve the same overall objectives.

Without constant effort on your part, departments will segregate themselves into silos. News directors will seek ratings without regard to the fact that news is funded by advertising sales. General sales managers will seek the most revenue possible, even though jamming too many spots in a newscast lowers ratings. Creative services will produce creative spots that look and feel great but don't necessarily advance the strategic plan. The chief engineer will set capital priorities without input from the news director.

In short, everyone will go in whatever direction seems to benefit their department. Not only are station goals not achieved, turf wars take up significant time and energy, and the advantage of group problem-solving is completely lost.

Great general managers understand that an interconnected management team, where everyone is seeking to achieve the same goals, can only be achieved by active work on their part.

Summary

Department heads are key leaders who constantly make decisions that affect a station's success. Keeping them all on the same page, looking toward achieving the same vision, is one of a general manager's most essential roles.

Department heads are usually strong individuals who are motivated by personal advancement. Showing how working as a team will help achieve their personal goals is a primary tool for general managers to use. It is equally important for a general manager to understand each department head's individual motivations.

Sharing information, creating situations where department heads have to work together, and using other tools that promote interaction help build esprit de corps.

Left to their own devices, department heads will form silos that are only interested in their own department's goals.

Key Takeaways

- Great general managers always inspire others to share a vision of success.
- To be effective, department heads must function as a team.
- Sharing information, solving problems as a group, and demonstrating why group success leads to individual success are among the tools in a general manager's arsenal.
- Lack of shared vision always results in departmental silos.

7

OPERATIONAL SECTIONS

The next five chapters are devoted to specific departments within a television station. They are not designed to be all-encompassing but rather to give a broad overview of each department's responsibilities.

My apologies in advance to current general managers and department heads who will see the department descriptions as simplistic.

The goal of these chapters is not so much to provide in-depth knowledge as it is to outline the inherent cultural barriers that are present in any media organization. One of the largest barriers is simply the amount of time it takes to run a successful department. Overreliance on habits and industry norms is driven by a need to simply get everything done in the allotted time.

The operational chapters are also designed to show why natural conflict and competing goals are normal. No one should be surprised that without continuing leadership by the general manager, silos always develop.

8

NEWS

There was a time when a general manager could let the news director worry about news while the GM concentrated on other areas. It does not work like that anymore.

News is the essence of any network-affiliated television station, the most important and expensive product the station produces. A general manager who does not understand news does not understand the heart of the station's value. Saying "I came out of sales" is no longer an acceptable reason for lacking expertise in this critical area.

If you do not come from a news background, take the time to understand how a news department works, how decisions are made, the importance of anchors and talent, why ethics are so important, the impact of digital platforms, pretty much everything that matters. The best time to do this is while you are still a department head.

A general sales manager who wants to be a general manager is well advised to build a relationship with the news director, then constantly ask questions. Just sitting in a news director's office during a show yields a vast amount of knowledge, providing you do it on a regular basis. As a sales manager, you are a nonthreatening observer. Once you become a general manager, the dynamic changes because you are the boss. Far better to learn about news when you are just another department head.

Ultimately, a general manager is responsible for a station's news product, so a working knowledge is essential.

When thinking of product, do not limit yourself to television. News platforms, including social media, are now limitless. What works on television may not work well on mobile devices.

I am not suggesting the GM should make content or coverage decisions. Those are for the news director to decide. Once a GM makes a coverage decision, that GM is now running the news department. A news director who has been bigfooted on a coverage decision is in an impossible position. Every future decision is now subject to second-guessing. Instead of going with her gut, she has to ask herself the question, "What does the GM think?" This not only slows down the decision-making process, it leads to bad decisions.

The GM does need to understand why the news director is making decisions and how those decisions fit into the station's overall strategy. Asking a news director why she made a decision is fine; just make sure you are getting information, not second-guessing. If your news director cannot make good coverage decisions, you need a new news director.

This does not mean you, as the general manager, are not involved with news. News is so central to a station's success that the general manager must have an appropriate level of involvement. That means diving deep into strategy, talent selection, department structure, budgeting, and other big-picture areas. The ability to have appropriate involvement without micromanaging is a fine line every general manager must walk. Great GMs often see themselves as partners with the news director and creative services director as they jointly create and implement big-picture strategy.

Most general managers come from sales, but that is not always the case. I came from a product and marketing background; many others come from the news director ranks, and some even come from engineering or finance.

If you are a general manager who came from news, you have to be especially diligent in limiting your role in the news department. Anyone who has been in the business awhile has a story about a news director who became a general manager yet could not let go of the news department. I often advise new general managers to try to stay away from the daily operations of whatever department they came from, be it news, sales, or any other area. Sure, you know more about that job than the department head currently in it, but you now have a new job. Let the department head learn, grow, and make decisions and even small mistakes. Your job is to provide guidance.

In order to know how to give guidance to a news director, you must know more than the mechanics. You must also understand the cultural and industry factors that affect every part of a newscast.

How News Directors Think

We live in an era of radical change, a time when all of us need to reexamine our opportunities, priorities, goals, and practices. You may be fortunate enough to have a news director who is doing these things, but that is rarely the case. Most news directors are simply too busy to think about advancing the brand. They have been raised in a system that encourages conformity and like-minded thinking. Some of this is good, but the trade-off is a system that rarely questions why and how decisions are made.

Because we are now in a multiplatform business, mobile, social media, and other distribution channels have made news instantaneous. Only original exclusive content provides any measure of control, and that is very little. A typical news director may be responsible for newscasts on multiple stations, apps, and other digital outlets, not the least of which is social media.

One would think that with all the new distribution opportunities, our product would now be tailored, but that is not always the case. Our business has become so homogenized, so afflicted with sameness, that new graduates of journalism schools are often already indoctrinated with old ideas the moment they graduate. Every new graduate knows how to do a stand-up, a package, and an example of anchoring. They also know how to put together a reel showing their performance, especially live shots. They also have a working knowledge of social media. Those things are not about journalism, and they are certainly not about differentiating product, but they are essential to getting a first job, so they take on an overwhelming importance.

Producers, from whose ranks news directors usually come, are equally indoctrinated with homogenized thinking. How to stack a newscast, how to structure blocks, how to back-time a show, how to post on the web—all the standard things. These are important skills but are regimented by sameness. Be it reporting, anchoring, or producing, students come out of school with a locked-in sense of how the business works. That sameness can easily continue throughout a person's career.

By the time a person gets to be a news director, she is completely harnessed into a culture that does not change. Sure, things are different around the edges from station to station, and new distribution opportunities appear almost daily, but for the most part, news directors think the same. You can take a good news director out of one station and put him or her in another without noticing any on-air content difference.

Pressure is another factor that leads to uniformity. It is not unusual for stations to produce up to six hours of news a day, more if you are a Fox affiliate. The only way to get that much news on the air is to structure it all the same way. New content in one newscast becomes regular content in the next. The live shot at the scene of a story eventually becomes a live shot at the same scene long after the story has ended.

All of this comes at the expense of actually thinking about the product. I sometimes say long-term planning to a news director is tonight's 11:00 p.m. show.

News is, of course, a highly competitive business, so news directors are also under pressure to match or beat the coverage of other stations. When one station goes on the air with exclusive breaking news, every other news director in the market freaks until they are also on the air from the same place with the same news.

When one station does do something different, such as adding a news crawl, every other news director feels compelled to copy the idea. In fact, crawls are a great example of sameness because most outlived their usefulness years ago, yet there are still stations in every market that run mundane news crawls across the bottom of the screen during newscasts. The same goes for putting the time and temperature on the screen. Time makes sense in the morning, but what sense does it make at 11:00 p.m.? It just reminds people how late it is.

Great news directors are also aggressive. There is a scene in the film *Broadcast News* that illustrates how our industry looks at aggressiveness. Holly Hunter plays a producer running breaking news coverage in Washington, DC. The network news president, who happens to be in town, is standing to the side along with the bureau chief listening to Hunter's character profanely rip into a photographer in the field. The president turns to the bureau chief and says, "I had no idea she was this good." I was working at the CBS affiliate in Washington when the movie came out. Several of us almost fell on the floor laughing because that scene so reflected the reality of our jobs.

Most importantly, news directors are under pressure to produce great ratings. As we discussed in the branding chapter, viewers choose favorite newscasts for complex reasons that go far beyond the content of a particular newscast. Nonetheless, news directors are the frontline managers held accountable for falling ratings. The pressure for numbers performance is immense.

When you add it all up, most news directors simply do not have the time to think about the big picture. The daily grind, along with the rubber band highs and lows that are inherent in the job, plus the pressure to produce numbers, take up all their time. This would only be of academic interest were it not for the real consequences of homogenization.

Add to this the fact viewers do not like radical change. They will punish a station that makes them uncomfortable. It seems every five years or so, a last-place station, looking for any Hail Mary pass that might work, announces they are going to reinvent local news. Maybe one of these experiments will someday work, but so far, the batting average is zero.

One of the things I learned from the *Ten O'Clock News with Carol Marin* experiment Pat Costello and I created in Chicago was that radical change must come from a market leadership position, not from the underdog, and even then it must be radical without looking radical.

Does Local News Really Have to Change?

Local news ratings have now been dropping steadily for multiple decades. Fragmentation, lifestyle changes, an overabundance of product, and viewer age are all factors, but I think the problem goes even deeper. Newscasts have become so structured, so predictable, that many younger potential viewers feel they are wasting their time.

Let's look at a common example. Suppose you live in Anytown, USA. A huge snowstorm is predicted for tomorrow, so you turn on a local station to get the forecast. Here is what you will likely see:

The newscast begins with two people at a desk who tell you in very serious tones that "severe weather is coming and chief meteorologist Judy Jones has more." We cut to Jones, who does about twenty seconds on the coming storm, then says, "I will have more later in the show."

Back to the anchors, who now throw live to reporter Bill Smith standing next to an interstate. Smith says, "Traffic is moving fine now, but that won't be the case tomorrow morning." Smith then goes to his package, which must contain the following elements: people buying milk, someone walking out of a hardware store with a new snow shovel, a pile of road salt, and of course, a guy sitting in a huge truck with the engine running.

After the package, we go back to Smith at the interstate, who is now joined by (and this is required) a state trooper. Smith says to the trooper, "What advice do you have for motorists tomorrow morning?" The trooper says, "Try to stay home, but if you have to get out, drive slowly." Smith then tosses back to the two anchors, who are nodding at this revelation.

Just when you think the live shot is over, one of the anchors says, "Bill, I have a question for the trooper." The anchor then asks his question, which is repeated by the reporter to the trooper.

I could go on, but you get the picture. Unfortunately, so does every viewer who just invested several minutes of their time yet got no new information. Instead, they were subjected to the same trite presentation they have heard a hundred times. It gets worse. Consumers who don't normally watch television news will tune in when severe weather is predicted. During the process of getting the information, all the reasons they do not normally watch local news are reinforced.

Research indicates weather is always the most important part of a newscast, but we also know many viewers tune in just to make sure they have not missed something important. If they see the standard "snow coverage" story, boring and with no genuinely new information, they feel free to go to their smartphone or iPad to immediately get the information the station's meteorologist has promised "later in the show."

Think now how this viewer scenario plays out on a slow news day. We are long past the time when viewers feel compelled to watch a boring newscast. Viewers tuning in to get the latest news, only to see the station lead with a live shot and a package about a minor community event, immediately realize nothing important is happening and turn off the set.

Many news directors still believe in the mantra of always leading with local, even if there is a bigger national or international story. This is another example of sameness the viewer inherently understands.

What if on that same day the station led with a minor community event and live shot, there was a major international story, such as a bombing that took several lives? That story would, of course, be in the newscast, but the station would most likely still lead with local news so the community event story came before the bombing story. The viewer, of course, already knows there was a bombing and is not willing to wait for the story to finally show up. The viewer either changes channels looking for the story or goes to her phone or tablet. The perception that local news is not worth investing her time in is reinforced.

Importance of Research

When talking about research, most television executives are referring to specific market studies commissioned by stations to understand station strengths and weaknesses, determine voids, and rank viewer approval of talent.

There are a number of companies that do a good job of researching a television market. Some are stronger than others, but the core information should be the same no matter who is doing the study.

The process usually begins by creating a questionnaire based on a boilerplate the research company provides. The cost of research varies greatly depending upon length and number of people interviewed. Most studies are targeted at twenty-five- through fifty-four-year-old viewers who watch a newscast at least twice a week.

News studies were originally in-home interviews back in the late 1950s, when Frank Magid started his company in Marion, Iowa. Over time, the expense of in-home interviews led to phone studies. Today, most studies are done over the internet, which offers the advantage of showing the consumer sound and video.

Once the study is complete, the research company writes a detailed report and an executive summary. Ideally, the researcher visits the station and makes a presentation to key managers. During the course of the presentation, additional questions are asked by the managers, hopefully giving an even fuller view of the information.

The problem with research is that managers often see it as the final word when in fact it is one important tool among many. Good news directors know their research well, but beware of a news director who says he or she makes every decision "according to the research."

Research is also a measurement of a point in time. Two-year-old research can be completely out of date.

In addition to commissioned studies, there are many other research tools, not the least of which are Nielsen and comScore. For better or worse, these companies are the umpires. Minute-by-minute studies, audience flow, and general consumer behavior research can all be helpful.

Research is an important tool, but assigning decisions to research only is a dangerous game to play. As the general manager, you need as much information from as many sources as possible, because at the end of the day, you have to take personal responsibility for station decisions.

Ethics Are Critical

Ethics are not just a nice thing to do. They are a business decision. They represent the core relationship between your news department and the consumers it serves.

Your entire station needs to know that you have a personal commitment to ethics, that you genuinely want to serve viewers and are determined to not allow any outside influencers, including advertisers, to damage your station's core commitment to always do the right thing. This is important because employees, especially those in the news department, need to understand you want to lead change for the right reasons. You will not destroy the wall between advertising and news for short-term gain.

If you work for a company that is willing to allow advertisers to dictate content, then good luck and stop reading right now. You are in a business that will never achieve market leadership in ratings, advertising, or profit.

I once took over a television station that had publicly lost its commitment to ethics. Everything that could possibly be sponsored was sponsored. Commercials were running over the closing news credits. Anchors were actually showing up in some paid commercials. Sales was clearly king, influencing content decisions across the board.

My first move was to cancel every news sponsorship. I then ended every relationship that prevented the station from making ethical decisions. Just as you cannot be a little pregnant, you cannot have ethics part of the time. The general sales manager became so discouraged by the things I was canceling he eventually tried to avoid coming in my office.

One year later, after we reaffirmed our commitment to ethics, canceled sponsorships, and even reduced the number of commercials in newscasts, the station had higher revenue than before the changes. You can sell your soul, but you are unlikely to get what it is really worth.

Think Like a Viewer

Because you are not part of producing the newscast, you have the advantage of trying to watch the news from a viewer's perspective. This is difficult because all of us are part of a system that is highly regimented and hard to change.

As you watch the newscast, ask yourself if what you see is advancing the station's strategic goals. Ask yourself what the purpose of various segments is. Why are they there? Do they actually help tell the story, or do they simply remind viewers why they don't watch television news?

After asking yourself these questions, ask the news director. As I said earlier, try not to second-guess, but still be frank. You want a discussion that will lead to a better newscast that will further the station's goals.

An understanding of the station's research can be invaluable when talking with the news director and creative services director. Research gives you specific markers that are helpful in understanding how viewers see your product and what they value. Just make sure research is only part of your arsenal.

Talent

No aspect of a news director's job is more difficult than dealing with talent. No matter how normal they look or act, no matter how long they have been in the business, no matter the market size, anchors and other talent are subject to a kind of pressure no one else in the station experiences.

Imagine if everywhere you went, no matter what place, what time or day, most of the people whom you saw or interacted with recognized you. Not only that, some of those people stopped to tell you how much they liked you, how impressed they were to meet you. If that sounds like a good thing, think again.

Being on television affects every relationship you have, influences every person you meet. The constant message from the public is that you have value because you are on television.

You and I have value because we have individual souls and are made in the image of God. We have inherent worth simply because we are human beings, not because of our jobs or other circumstances. But if you are constantly told that the real reason you have value is because of your job, over time that ongoing reinforcement will affect you. Is your good friend really your good friend, or is it really about your job? Does anyone like you for yourself, or is it just about being on television? Who can you believe? Who can you trust?

Because you are constantly on display, you completely lose anonymity. You always have to look presentable. You have to be careful how you speak to people, what you say to clerks, how you register a complaint with a business, all the everyday things in life we take for granted—even honking your horn at someone.

Anchors in good-sized markets are well paid, but rarely do they earn the kind of money members of the public might think. No anchor wants to admit this, so they feel pressured to drive the right kinds of cars and live in the right neighborhoods whether they can afford it or not.

Because their jobs have become so personalized, anchors take anything that negatively affects their performance personally. Poor writing, a burned-out key light, even a technical error can set some off, causing their fellow workers to see them as arrogant.

More than once, I've seen anchors ask engineers to soften cameras so the lines in their faces will become less obvious.

Now think what all this means when ratings start to go down. Most anchors look at the overnights daily. When the ratings go down, it is seen as personal. "Do people not like me anymore?" "Am I getting too old?" Suddenly, all those people looking at you in public places takes on new meaning. "Do they think I'm a failure?" "Why have they chosen to stop watching me?"

Paranoia is an occupational disease. "Will that younger, more attractive weekend anchor get my job?" "The general manager didn't smile when she passed me in the hall this afternoon." "My contract is up in three months and no one has spoken to me! Am I about to lose my job?"

Add to all this the internal conflict some anchors experience over their journalist versus performance roles. Dan Rather always kidded himself that he earned millions every year because he was a journalist. Journalism had little to do with it. Other people produced the journalism. Dan performed. Knowing how strongly he felt about this, during an event in Chicago, I once introduced Dan by talking about his long reporting career from the Kennedy assassination to Saddam Hussein's invasion of Kuwait. I talked about how Dan was a reporter's reporter, which he had been. When I turned around, Dan was in tears. He later told me it was the best introduction he had ever had. Why? Because it reinforced the way he wanted things to be, not the reality of who he really was.

Anchors are people, but they are also assets. The inescapable fact is they must attract a sufficient number of viewers to justify the investment your station is making in them. No matter how much you may personally like or dislike an anchor, his or her commercial value and paychecks are based on Nielsen ratings.

To a lesser extent, the issues anchors deal with extend to every other person who earns their living by being on television.

The business can be especially hard on reporters, whose salaries don't come close to matching anchor pay, which is why they tend to be so young. There is an incredible surplus of young journalism graduates entering the market every year. Most never get a job. Those who do make it often find something else to do after a few years.

Any news director will tell you that a large part of their time is spent dealing with the people problems every newsroom faces. Under the best of conditions, it can be challenging.

As the general manager, one of your responsibilities is to help lower the fear level that is often just below the surface for all talent. Just stopping by to say hello, smiling, and giving small but sincere compliments go a long way with someone in a job that is by nature insecure.

Of course, your role dealing with talent goes far beyond making them feel secure. These are people whose performances have a material effect on station ratings, so you have a stake in their success. There are times when you have to be frank, especially about performance issues that need to be corrected. There are times when talent will try to go around the news director. When that happens, they need to learn the news director has your support.

The news director also needs your support in talent contract negotiations. Sometimes you play the role of closer, helping get a new deal signed. Other times you play the part of a hard bargainer. It all depends on the individual negotiation.

There are a couple of things to keep in mind when dealing with contracts. First, do your best to treat everyone the same. There are no secrets in a newsroom. If you agree to your main anchor's demand he be given an extra week of vacation, you will now have everyone asking for an extra week. It is essential you be able to look people in the eye and say, "We don't do that." Or, "I'm sorry. This is a fair offer and our top number."

It is also important to not become so focused on getting someone to sign a new deal that he or she becomes a problem employee once it has been signed. I often say to talent before finalizing a tough negotiation, "Don't sign this deal unless you can feel good about it."

There are also times when you have to push someone to reach an agreement. I remember one time when a morning meteorologist kept putting off signing his contract. The news director was at his wits' end. I finally said, "Bring him over to my office." When they walked in, I stood up, shook the meteorologist's hand, and said, "I'm so sorry to learn you will be leaving. You have my best wishes on whatever you do in the future."

"What!" he exclaimed. "I'm not leaving!"

I put a surprised look on my face and said, "I was told you didn't want to sign your deal, so I assumed you were leaving. Is that not the case?"

He ran out of my office, got the contract from his desk, signed it, and brought it right back.

You also have to be consistent in enforcing noncompetes. This can be tricky because you don't want to end up in court facing the possibility of a judge negating all noncompetes. For the most part, stations respect other stations' noncompetes. My personal view is that a signed contract should be fully honored by both parties. I once kept an anchor off the air for a full year after he left us to go to another station. He got a job selling cars to support his family. I didn't do this to be mean. I did it because everyone else needed to know we enforced noncompetes.

The most important link you have with viewers is through talent. They are critical to the success of your station and, therefore, well worth the time and effort you invest in them.

Hiring a News Director

Hiring the right news director is one of the most important

things you will do as a general manager. I've hired my share over the years, sometimes making great decisions, sometimes making the wrong decisions.

Character can be a good starting place. Obviously, you are looking for news skills, leadership ability, and vision, but it is extremely difficult to find all these attributes in one person. Like the rest of us, news directors learn as they go, making both great decisions and mistakes. By starting with character, you will get a person willing to learn from mistakes.

Anchors, reporters, and other on-air people are extremely difficult to manage. They do not respond well to someone who is dictatorial, nor do they respond to the other end of the spectrum. What do they respond to? Someone who is in charge and willing to make decisions but also willing to hear from other people.

Obviously, you are going to seek someone who is compatible with your management style, but you also need someone who will always tell you the truth, not throwing others under the bus yet also not defending bad decisions. Character is essential.

Summary

News is central to a brand's success. Great general managers understand and are involved with news strategy, the importance of talent, ethics, and other critical news functions. That does not mean they micromanage the news department. They are partners with the news director in the big picture.

Because news directors are under such intense pressure to get product both on the air and on multiple other platforms, they naturally concentrate on the daily tasks. It is up to the general manager to take the lead in looking to the future.

Audience fragmentation, changing lifestyles, and needs of younger consumers mean television news must move beyond the standardized, predictable presentation consumers are so used to seeing. This must come incrementally because consumers hate radical change. The key is to create radical change that is introduced slowly but nonetheless changes the paradigm.

Research is an important tool, but it provides only one dimension. It must be used carefully.

Because of the unique pressure of their jobs, talent can be difficult to work with. Understanding those pressures, and how anchors react to them, is an important management tool worth taking the time to learn.

Successful news departments are grounded by ethical attitudes and practices. Ignoring the importance of ethics leads to peril.

Key Takeaways

- News is far too important for a general manager not to be involved. This does not mean the general manager fills the news director's role.
- Newscasts are homogenized in part because news directors have too much to do and are under such extreme pressure to succeed that they are forced to rely on habits. It is up to the general manager to think about the future.
- Research is important, but research does not take the place of making decisions.
- Ethics are a business decision.

9

CREATIVE SERVICES

To fully understand news, a general manager must also understand creative services.

Of all the departments in a television station, the role of creative services is usually the most misunderstood. Originally known as the "promotion department," over the years, the area has been known by a number of titles ranging from "advertising and promotion" to "marketing."

The best way to think of creative services is as an in-house advertising agency whose only client is the television station. They are a critical player in both the formulation and execution of the station's strategic plan; they are responsible for both on-air and outside advertising.

Great creative services departments are involved in every element of a station's brand, from promo content to graphic and set design. The "creative services" moniker is unfortunate because it makes the department sound like a group of people who sit around thinking of the next great idea, and some departments do just that. But the best creative services directors understand that marketing must be done within the context of the station's strategic plan, thus always furthering the brand. Anything that does not further the brand muddles the brand.

One of the great problems we have in television is our desire for the next big idea, the next impressive visual effect, the latest exciting fad. The result can be an unfocused station that is everything, but nothing. This is usually evidenced by promos that might look great on an individual basis but carry no central theme or clear, consistent viewer benefit. Viewer benefits must be constantly reinforced. Otherwise, they become lost in the clutter.

To be fair, very few companies have the discipline required to stick to a strategic plan in their advertising. Commercials that win awards are usually funny or otherwise cutting edge. Rarely are they judged on effectiveness. Look no further than the Super Bowl to see this play out. The commercials we remember are usually the most creative and attention grabbing. If they are funny, so much the better. What we rarely remember is why they might make us want to buy a product.

None of this is to say promos should not be creative. If they are to stand out, they must be creative, interesting, and well done. But to be effective, they must constantly reinforce the station's brand in a way that motivates viewers.

Coordination with News

To be effective, news and creative services must stay on the same page. That begins with the relationship between the news director and the creative services director. Each must respect and be willing to consult with the other on a daily basis.

I've found it helpful to have a short meeting every weekday morning with the news director, creative services director, chief engineer, and other managers as appropriate. The purpose is to keep everyone on the same page and solve problems before they start. As we will discuss in the engineering chapter, the nature of engineering often creates conflict with the news and creative services departments, which is why it is helpful to include engineering in the daily operations meeting.

Not only should the news director and creative services director be on the same page, so should their staffs. In fact, many stations house their topical promo producer in the news department.

Branding Campaigns

If you have read this far, you know that a station's brand is determined by consumers, not the station. Unfortunately, many stations do not understand this basic concept, thinking a brand is a catchy phrase reinforced by advertising. The search for the perfect descriptive line that will motivate viewers can easily obscure the need for advertising to reflect the station's real brand, not a hope or a wish.

As we discussed earlier, the search for the perfect branding line usually begins with research to identify voids. These voids are then paired with a station's perceived ability to fulfill a particular void. This is often followed by testing to determine the best line. Sometimes testing does reveal the perfect descriptive line, but that is rare. Unfortunately, stations usually seem compelled to have some kind of line no matter what, so they choose either the highest-testing one or something they just plain like. Over the following years, the station will invest a fortune in airtime repeating this line, not just in promos but over and over in newscasts. Not only is this effort often wasted, it means the station is missing the opportunity to build an effective brand.

My biggest gripe with most brands built on hope and product change is that very little else usually changes. Stations hate to give anything up, so the new advertising brand is something else added to the mix. Rarely is anything given up to make room for the new branding line. I've seen stations with remnants of up to a dozen past brands still evident on the station.

By now, you must think I hate brand lines. I don't. A great

line that accurately reflects the unique reasons consumers love a station is a great benefit and well worth having. The problem is that most lines are contrivances hoping to somehow influence viewers through advertising alone.

The best creative services directors understand what brand is and is not. If your creative services director is stuck in the past, give him the help he needs to understand the real value of his work.

Just as a general manager is ultimately responsible for the news product, the same is true with creative services.

Relationship with News

Some stations choose to put creative services under the news director. I disagree with this approach because it assumes creative services is subservient to news. The best creative services directors spend a great deal of time with their news directors, especially when it comes to watching the product. Because of their strong relationship, those creative services directors are able to raise ideas and make suggestions about every aspect of the newscast.

Because the creative services director is also responsible for graphics, sets, lighting, and other important support services, the CSD is in a position to also advance the product.

Respect

No matter how good a creative services director you have, that person can only function at full speed if you give him or her the same respect you do other department heads.

Because of the nature of their job, creative services directors are sometimes seen as "just creative" or somehow less important than sales managers or news directors. Properly used, a creative services director is a critical member of your management team. Always treat him or her that way.

Summary

Creative services functions as an in-house advertising agency whose primary responsibility is to make sure the brand is reflected in every part of the marketing, product, and related areas.

Unfortunately, creative services has a history of concentrating more on great ideas and production value than discipline of the brand. Creativity must work within the guideposts of the brand. Anything that does not advance the brand works against the brand.

The relationship between news and creative services is essential to a station's success. If the news director and creative services director are not on the same page, the brand suffers.

For many years, news and sales were the most important departments in a television station. They still are, but a proper understanding of the role creative services plays elevates the value of that department and helps gain the respect creative services directors deserve.

Key Takeaways

- Creative services is the keeper of the brand.
- Creativity must function within the brand.
- News and creative services must function as a unit.
- Creative services is a key department, not just a support group.

10

SALES

Like news and marketing, sales is one of the key areas that determine a station's success.

If you did not come out of sales, investing the time it will take to understand the nuances is well worth the effort. I'm not suggesting you have to be an expert or second-guess your general sales manager, but unless you dig into the details, you can't fully understand your station's sales strategy. Like news, the days of simply saying "I have a great sales manager who handles that area" are far behind us. You are ultimately responsible for the success of your sales department.

The Big Picture

No station department is under greater attack than sales. Every national brand, led by Google and Facebook, is seeking to capitalize on incredibly lucrative local markets. Moreover, new local competitors are popping up daily... and not just in media. Any activity that uses time, any activity that costs the consumer money, any activity that solves a consumer need is a threat.

Because new brand threats are arising so quickly, the temptation is to either ignore the threat or throw your hands up in frustration. Either of those would be a terrible mistake.

No matter what form it takes, local revenue is the key to a local station's future. For many years, revenue was split evenly between local and national at around 50 percent each. That began to change during the early 2000s as new national competitors entered the picture. Today, national is a significantly smaller percentage of business and dropping. The problem is that the structure of national advertising, no matter what form of media, is commodity based, making it much more difficult to use quality and user relationships to compete. National will always be a part of our mix, but local is clearly the future. By local, I do not just mean television spot advertising. Mobile, web, OTT, and other platforms are becoming more important every day.

The irony of local is that a good percentage of the newspaper advertising that went away with the demise of daily papers never found a home. Small local businesses used to be able to buy newspaper ads with confidence they would reach target consumers. Today, those small businesses are caught up in a complex world of choices that may or may not work.

Back in the day when television was only about commercials on a traditional television channel, spot advertising was simply too expensive for small clients. Today's local arsenal of products, not the least of which are the multiplexed D2 channels that target subaudiences, means stations are in a position to serve new kinds of clients with cost-effective solutions. As new platforms continue to emerge, so will sales opportunities. The important thing is not to be caught in the old paradigm of thinking spot is so big, television is so important, other platforms are simply additive. No one knows what platform will dominate in the future.

Why Brand Matters in Sales

There are a few examples of newspapers around the country that are doing a great job of trying to rebuild their brands for a new time and new audiences, but in most markets, the void left by newspapers is real, not only in content but also advertising. Because there is consumer need for both of those things, someone will fill the void. Moreover, there are other local information voids, especially among younger consumers, that have never been serviced by either newspaper or television. This is in part because each generation defines news differently from the last. That does not mean these consumers have no interest in news. It means their interests, as they define news, are not being served by traditional media.

Television news, as it is presently configured, is not likely to serve the information needs of younger consumers. Because of the cultural barriers we have previously discussed, most television newscasts will never serve those age groups. This is why conversion from platform thinking to brand thinking is so critical.

Given the cultural barriers to change, why would we continue to think of local television as the base for a brand-based business? Why not simply devote all our efforts to 5G or some other modern technology? The answer is that television is the last form of mass media—the only one still standing. In short, there are no other candidates. No other form of media has the existing local consumer relationships television enjoys. However, television continues to be a fragmenting platform. It should be used as a launchpad now, not down the line when it may not be as strong.

Just because younger viewers do not regularly watch television news does not mean they have no relationships with their local television stations. Young consumers will tell you they depend on television for emergency weather information, big story coverage, major network programming, and some level of local and national sports. The basis of a brand relationship with these consumers already exists—not for every station but certainly for one or two in each market.

Think what it would mean to sales revenue if a television station became the leading local brand in a larger sense. Consider the value of younger consumers, whether they regularly watch television news or not, seeing a local station as the most important resource for their definition of local news. Not only would there still be opportunity for traditional sales, including the targeting inherent in ATSC 3.0, but opportunities for advertising and direct consumer payments would be unlimited. Moreover, the client base for such a brand would be wider and deeper than anything we have now. Using a leading television station as a powerful base to becoming the leading local brand is the best thing that could possibly happen to future advertising revenue.

But what of today? Though mobile, web, multiplexed channels, and other opportunities for revenue are already being monetized and will grow, for the moment the bulk of station revenue continues to be television spot advertising, particularly local spot with emphasis on local direct.

Great sales departments are organized to take advantage of both the traditional revenue and new platform revenue available right now, but we need to think beyond today. As we look to future content products, we need to think also about how those products will be monetized. Building a relationship with specific consumer groups is only of value if we also learn how to serve their needs in ways that benefit us financially. We need to also be open to completely different ways of monetizing future content, especially direct consumer payments either as subscriptions or specific product sales.

As we saw in the "News" chapter, in order to create the future, you must first become today's local news leader. The same is true in sales. Launching the future means first becoming the leader in current revenue. That means having the best sales leaders, best management and support groups, best sales team in your market. Great sales teams not only sell "beyond the numbers" but they are far more likely to monetize new ideas than less talented groups.

The following sections offer a practical guide for the way television sales departments function because the opportunities of tomorrow will be built on the successes of today. As you read, think also in terms of today's cultural barriers and how to change them into opportunities for the future.

Again, my apologies if you have a sales background and find this simplistic or lacking important points.

Overview

Like everything else in local television, the sales process is competitive. Great salespeople love the thrill of a close, the pursuit of a bigger share, the financial scorecard that determines winners and losers. On average, good salespeople usually earn more than their counterparts in other departments, which is another form of motivation.

Back in the days when television had no real competitors, sales departments gained a reputation for high living. So much money was coming in that no one had to work very hard. Any retired sales executive from that era has a bagful of stories about the lifestyle many of them lived.

Understand that in spite of the old stories, which still linger, that era is long gone. Today's sales departments are professional, buttoned down, and hardworking. With multiple platforms to sell and new competitors on all sides, the process of closing sales is complex and challenging. Strong sales executives are well compensated, but they also earn those dollars.

In theory, there should be a direct correlation between ratings and revenue. The reality is stations' ratings and revenue rarely match. The relationship between ratings and revenue is based on holding capacity, a measurement of the financial value of a station's ratings compared to that of every other station in the market. Great sales departments always outperform their holding capacity. That means a station could be number three in ratings yet rank number two in revenue. It also means a first-place station could also be first in revenue but still not perform up to its holding capacity.

A first-place station whose revenue does not exceed holding capacity has a problem. If ratings and revenue matched, then why have a sales department at all? Clerks could do the job. Great sales departments always outperform their ratings. Poor sales departments do not live up to ratings.

How does a sales department outperform ratings? By "selling beyond the numbers." That means understanding a station's audience and how that audience matches a client's needs. In order to do that, sales departments employ a wide range of tools, such as lifestyle research, combining multiple platforms to solve a specific client's needs, incentive packages, and other tools. At the end of the day, a salesperson's greatest asset is his or her own drive and belief in the product he or she is selling.

One of a general manager's most important jobs is to make sure the sales department believes in the product. Just as belief is essential to building news ratings, it is an equally critical motivator to account executives.

Demographic Ratings

Television advertising sales are based primarily on demographic ratings.

The primary job of the Nielsen Station Index is to provide household and demographic ratings information to both television stations and advertising companies. Nielsen uses measurement panels of viewers to gain this information. These panels are designed to be a sample of the overall viewing universe.

Methodology and technology are constantly changing, but all involve some form of panel or sample households. Ideally, Nielsen would like to use "people meters," measuring which family members are watching which shows in real time, in all households, but lower revenue totals in smaller markets means Nielsen employs other methods, though Nano meters are their current first choice.

A second company, comScore, determines ratings based on set satellite and cable box activity. comScore does not measure over-the-air usage, nor does it have specific demographic measuring tools; therefore, comScore's demographics are "imputed"— that is, estimated. Nielsen has also used the imputed method in some markets.

The problem with both Nielsen and comScore is that panel measurement is not an exact measurement, only an estimate. Digital platforms, such as mobile, offer measurement of true usage. As the television industry transitions to the ATSC 3.0 standard, audience measurement will eventually become far more accurate.

Audience measurement technology and methodology are constantly changing, so by the time you read this, a deep dive into the inner workings of the measurement services might be out of date. The important thing to remember is that advertising is only valuable if a client can be assured their message will reach their desired audience.

Why Demographics Matter

Most consumer products are bought by adults between the ages of twenty-five and fifty-four; therefore, this demographic group is usually considered the most valuable audience any television station can have. Breaking it down even further, women between the ages of twenty-five and fifty-four make far more product-buying decisions than men; therefore, female demos are usually more valuable than male demos.

This does not mean other age groups are not important. If you take the time to think about what groups a particular program might appeal to and then look at the commercials in that program, you will get an idea of how demographics ratings are used.

It is possible for a leading television station to win household ratings but lose demographic ratings. When this happens, remember that bragging rights do not count for much.

Advertising Agencies

Large advertisers, such as national brands like Ford, use agencies to purchase advertising. It is not unusual for a client to use one agency for creating commercials and another to place advertising. Agencies that only place advertising are known as time buyers.

Local advertisers may or may not use advertising agencies. Some businesses use agencies because they like the simplicity of not having to deal with the intricacies of demographic targeting, ad schedule placement, and negotiation.

One of the oddities of time buyers is that the people making buying decisions are often young and not highly paid. A twenty-five-year-old could be placing millions of dollars' worth of advertising yet make a much smaller salary than the commission-based salespeople calling on her.

One of the first things I learned on becoming a general manager was that time spent with buyers was always a good investment. Taking buyers to top restaurants and other venues they could not afford on their own usually paid off in higher revenue shares. When buyers talk about having a "relationship" with a station, it usually means they are on very good terms with that station's account executive and possibly both the general manager and the general sales manager. It also means the buyer is regularly taken to expensive lunches or dinners by the account executive.

When a buyer talks about a station being "easy to work with," they mean the station sells them advertising at a below-market price. A "hard-to-work-with" station is one that is constantly pushing for higher prices.

Lest you get the idea buyers are just interested in lunches and pricing, there are other factors that can be much more important. Sometimes an advertising schedule bought at too low a price is "bumped out" by higher-paying customers and does not run. Other times, individual spots are bumped for other reasons, but regardless of why a spot does not air, a "make good" must be scheduled by the account executive. Make goods that are not placed in a timely manner, or schedules that do not run properly, matter much more than an expensive lunch or tickets to a ball game.

An agency buying service makes money by charging a commission, normally 15 percent, to the television stations receiving the buy. A $100,000 buy would mean the agency would receive a $15,000 commission, netting the station $85,000.

When large advertisers do not use an ad agency or a buying service, it is usually because the advertiser wants to receive the 15 percent commission themselves. This is called taking the buy in-house.

Buying Mechanics

Here's how the sales process works. A buyer might send an e-mail to various stations saying she is planning to spend $20,000 for a specific client and product. She will include a target demo, say, women ages twenty-five through fifty-four, and the dates she expects the schedule to run. She may also suggest a cost per point (CPP) she expects to pay. For the purpose of this illustration, let's say she is willing to pay $25 per demo point rating for women ages eighteen through forty-nine and would like the schedule to run in the afternoon news. If a station is currently producing a

4.2 demo rating in afternoon news, the buyer would like to pay $105 per spot (4.2 × 25 = 105). This process is called sending out avails, meaning the buyer is asking for availability of times and pricing in the demographics and time of day she has specified. She will also give start and end dates for the schedule.

Armed with this information, each station then submits a suggested schedule using the parameters the buyer has set. Some stations will think the suggested CPP is too low, or they may believe their ratings are going to be higher than whatever past rating period the buyer is using. As a result, station submissions may be very different from what the buyer has suggested. Now the negotiation begins.

Television stations are not allowed to coordinate their submissions with competing stations in any way. However, the buyer is perfectly free to share any information she wants. Once all submissions are in hand, the time buyer tries to play each station off the others. She may say to one station, "You are asking $28 per point, but your competitor WXXX is only asking $23 per point. You need to drop your price." The buyer may or may not be telling the truth.

You see the problem. The salesperson must make an educated guess about what CPP and number of demo points the buyer is actually willing to accept. The salesperson's past experience with this particular buyer, his sense of what other buyers are paying, his observations of what competitors have been willing to accept in the past, his view of current market demand, and analysis of his station's available inventory all play parts in making a pricing decision.

It is also important to understand that the salesperson does not set station advertising rates. The general sales manager, usually in conjunction with the local and national managers, makes those decisions. If pricing was left to the salespeople, they would lower prices to increase their share of a buy. Because they are paid a commission, the larger their share of the buy, the more money they personally make. It is critical to understand this basic of our business. Salespeople are motivated to get the highest share possible. That means lower ad rates. Salespeople are understandably motivated by their own self-interest, which is why managers must approve each submission before it is actually proposed to an agency.

Typically, the general sales manager will reset rates at least once a week, specifying the lowest rate the station is currently willing to accept for each demo point in each time period. Armed with that information and feedback from the buyer, the salesperson is now set to negotiate the buy. Negotiation is never just about price. A salesperson's relationship with the buyer, the station's market position, and the station's reputation for timely handling of make goods all play parts. The buyer's demand for guaranteeing ratings performance is also important.

Once the buyer completes her purchases, she will typically tell each buyer what their "share of the buy" was. Many will also tell each station what share every other station was given. Again, the station has no way of knowing if this information is correct. It often is, but some buyers are not above manipulating the information in ways they believe will affect the next advertising buy.

After the schedule runs, the buyers will "post the buy." Using the ratings data for the period during which the schedule ran, the buyer will compare each station's performance to see if the projected ratings were obtained. If they were, the buy "posts," and everyone moves on to the next buy. However, if the buy "does not post," both the buyer and the station have a problem. The buyer cannot afford to have her client think she overpaid, so she will immediately demand the station "add weight," meaning to run enough additional commercials at no charge to bring the buy into compliance with the original agreement, thus "making up the weight."

If the station is not able to make up the weight, bad things happen. The station that failed to make up weight is either left off the next buy or sees a much lower share of future buys.

Here's a real example. The 1998 Nagano Olympics was one of the lowest rated of all time. As a result, the CBS-owned station I was running owed American Airlines over $1 million in makeup weight. There was simply no way to make up that much weight in a reasonable time period. For the following two years, the station was excluded from every American ad buy. Our general sales manager did everything in her power to satisfy the client. We even offered them a prime-time special, but to no avail. This is an extreme example, but it shows what can happen when ratings guarantees are not met.

Selling advertising to ad agency buyers is an interesting proposition: part information gathering, part analysis, part actual selling, all complicated by the fact the advertising must actually work.

Local versus National

Television stations usually break down spot sales into two areas: local and national. The names are descriptive of the categories.

Local, usually the larger share of advertising sales, is sold by a team of local account executives overseen by a local sales manager. Local account executives, also known as local reps, are responsible for selling advertising both to local advertising agencies and directly to local advertisers. They are also selling other platforms such as mobile, web and multiplexed D2 channels. Clients range from smaller merchants to larger advertisers, such as car dealers. Some local advertisers use agencies to make their buys, some have in-house agencies, and some use neither.

Selling directly to a local advertiser is called local direct. Local direct clients are usually individual merchants who buy directly from the television station without a middleman. These clients often buy based on what they actually see on the local stations, meaning quality of product can become as strong a selling point as audience size.

Of the various ways to sell local advertising, the preferred method is usually local direct. Not only are direct sales to a local business less price sensitive (since these kinds of advertisers rarely deal with ratings), but if the local client has not previously used television, their initial business will often be exclusive to the station, a 100 percent share.

The best local account executives understand their job is to not just sell advertising but to help the client achieve business goals. That means becoming a resource to the client, even advising the client how to spend the rest of their advertising budget. In the best of these relationships, everyone benefits. The television station gets the largest share of the client's business, and the client gets valuable help implementing their marketing plan without having to hire an advertising agency.

As discussed earlier, the process of dealing with advertising agencies, even local ones, is much more price sensitive. However, the process is also influenced by the fact local buyers live in their markets and watch local television stations, a factor that naturally affects buyer perceptions and, therefore, pricing and share. If a buyer loves watching a particular morning newscast, that newscast will naturally be "on the buy."

Role of the National Rep

An agent or representative company, known as the rep firm or simply the rep, normally sells national advertising for a station. The rep normally deals with a station's national sales manager.

Representative companies are in business because it does not make economic sense for a local television station to maintain offices in major advertising centers, such as New York, Chicago, and Detroit, not to mention important regional advertising centers, such as Atlanta and Dallas. By representing multiple television stations, the rep is able to maintain offices in key markets across the company.

It is not unusual for larger groups of television stations to create in-house rep firms to serve their stations, thus lowering costs. The downside of owning your own rep firm is that you can't change firms if you are unhappy with your current one's performance. Ask six group heads their thoughts on outside- versus company-owned rep firms and you will likely get six different answers. Like so many other things in television, there is not a single right or wrong answer.

Given the lack of connection between national advertising buyers and the far-flung markets they buy, national is understandably more price sensitive than local. National sales managers work hard to develop relationships with these buyers by regular visits and expensive lunches and dinners. As a GM, it is always worth the effort to spend time with buyers.

It has been my experience that most general managers rarely make sales calls. I think that is a mistake. Showing up at a buyer's office or taking her to lunch allows you to tell your station's story without the pressure of actually selling something. Most buyers are relatively young and not highly paid. They are often impressed by a personal visit from the station's top executive. I always make a point of writing my cell number on my card and urging them to call me if they ever have a complaint.

Pricing and Inventory Control

Television advertising is a perishable product that has no value past its sell-by date. However, that does not mean a station should be "sold out." The sold-out condition means a station's advertising has been underpriced. It also means inadequate inventory is leftover for marketing the station's own newscasts and programs.

Years ago when I arrived as the new general manager of a large market station, I discovered advertising was sold out, yet we were not making budget. It didn't take a genius to figure out we had a pricing problem. I eventually had to terminate both the general sales manager and the local sales manager.

Over the years, I've heard many excuses for being sold out without making budget but none that is acceptable. Here are some of the more popular excuses I've heard from general sales managers.

• We didn't make budget because the leading station sells too low. We have to match their pricing.
• The market is soft, so everybody is dropping prices.
• We make sure to fill up at the beginning of the month, then preempt the cheap stuff later on.
• Ratings are down, so we had no choice.
• We have to price for share.

None of these excuses is acceptable. They all say the same thing: the general sales manager has no confidence in the station's product or his or her ability to sell. If your general sales manager is giving these kinds of excuses, or the dozen or so others in the same vein, it's time to take a hard look at the sales department.

A good place to start is comparing pricing and sellout by daypart. For instance, if there is demand for morning news, how is that time period priced? Is there a wide disparity in pricing within the same daypart? What does the average unit rate look like? Is the station sold out in some areas yet wide open in others? Simply blaming demand is not a reasonable excuse. We pay managers and account executives high levels of compensation for selling, not just taking orders.

Once you understand inventory and pricing, it's time to find out how strong the local sales staff is. How many top performers are driving the station? Are others barely getting by? If so, why?

The bottom line is that sales has the great advantage of being measured objectively. If appropriate goals are not being achieved, then you need to know why.

Commercial Loads

Determining length and placement of commercial breaks in local news is both a science and an art. Science because we know how breaks interact with Nielsen rules. Art because there is no absolute best number of breaks or number of spots in a break.

What we do know is that overly long commercial breaks cause viewers to turn off or go to another station. Breaks that are too frequent do the same thing. How long is too long? Different stations and companies have different policies. One station might believe no internal news break should be over 2:30, while another may believe 3:30 is fine. Shorter breaks are obviously better, but there are no hard-and-fast rules.

Over the years, I've participated in any number of newscast commercial inventory experiments. One thing I've learned is that a newscast without any commercial breaks at all is a bad idea. Commercial breaks give viewers a chance to breathe. And while viewers hate some commercials, others are seen as providing helpful information. From a brand perspective, commercials are part of the overall product, so they also play a small part in station perception.

One of the great conundrums in our business is whether or not running a commercial break at the top of late news hurts the newscast's ratings. The answer seems obvious. Of course it hurts ratings. But does it? Minute-by-minute audience flow studies show most people who leave change channels or turn off the set during network closing credits or after seeing the beginning of the newscast, not during a 1:00 station break. Most stations do not run a break in front of late news because they think it must cause some viewers to tune out. I agree with this philosophy, but I also must say the data does not support it.

Commercials are important to ratings because they affect audience flow and retention, which sometimes creates friction between the news and sales departments. As the general manager, you are the arbiter, so this is an area you must understand.

There are also times of year, such as just before an election, where it makes sense to temporarily increase inventory in news. There are other times, when demand is light or in an important ratings period (even though demos are year round, some periods remain more important than others), when it makes sense to increase news content by decreasing inventory. In any case, these are decisions you must sign off on. They are too important to be left to the sales manager.

Digital

Unlike spot, where audience is estimated, mobile, web, and other forms of digital revenue have the advantage of actual audience measurement. This makes the agency selling process different because clients know exactly what they will get for their money.

Digital opportunities, especially mobile, are constantly expanding. The use of third-party advertising means even stations with weak product of their own have ways to put valuable inventory in front of clients.

Most digital clients are also television clients, but not in all cases. Digital is not limited to a Designated Marketing Area (DMA) or other geography. A digital client could be out of a station's normal business area. Another client might be too small to afford television but can afford a digital product.

The great thing digital advertising offers is the opportunity to create new products and new selling opportunities for all-size clients, including those too small to afford traditional television.

Because digital platforms do not use the public airways for transmission, the constant Federal Communications Commission (FCC) oversight that marks broadcast channels is not present in digital media, which represents additional opportunity.

In some sales departments, digital sales managers report to local sales managers, but that has become less the case. Strong digital sales managers deserve to be on par with both the local and national managers.

Multichannel Revenue

Because spot revenue represents such a large percentage of station billing, it is easy to overlook the real value of secondary networks, such as MeTV. These channels have real audiences with real value. As the general manager, you should know every day how well your sales department is monetizing every platform.

Traffic

Traffic is the process of creating the daily schedule, including commercial placement, for a television station. Traffic departments produce a daily station "log" which guides master control operators throughout the twenty-four hours of a broadcast day.

Most traffic departments are centralized operations that serve multiple stations. Specialized computer programs, such as WideOrbit, allow them to make complicated decisions regarding placement of commercials.

Traffic is a key component of customer service, so it is critical for you to know if yours is doing the best job possible. The sales manager's opinion is a logical place to start, but you should also ask clients if they are getting everything they expect from your station. Finally, get to know whoever is in charge of traffic for the group.

Credit and Collections

The selling process is not complete until someone collects the money. Every station gets regular reports listing clients whose bills have not been paid in a reasonable time. If a client is 90 days past due, that is a very bad sign. A wait of 120 days means you are probably never going to see the money.

Sooner or later, you will run across clients who are chronic late payers. Because of their tardiness, your company's appropriate financial people will eventually halt the client's advertising until the balance is paid. When that happens, it is not unusual for an account executive or manager to argue for leniency. Acquiescing is usually a bad idea. If you do not hold a client responsible for paying their bill on time, they will never be on time.

Lax enforcement of the rules puts the station at risk of losing multiple months' billing should a client declare bankruptcy or go out of business, something every veteran general manager has seen. Making special credit deals is rarely worth the risk.

Budgeting

It is impossible to determine what the state of the local economy will be six months in the future, much less twelve months down the line, but that is exactly what we try to do during the annual budgeting process. Surprisingly, companies often come close to getting it right.

The baseline for the coming year's budget is always the previous year. That year is, of course, still in progress during budget time, so the first goal is to estimate total revenue for the current year. Looking forward, some key factors include the local market economy; demographic ratings projections; special opportunities, such as the Super Bowl or Olympics; programming changes in the market; and, of course, past performance. Because the Olympics and national political races are biennial, budgeted revenue for an upcoming year is compared to both the current year and the previous one.

Projecting revenue is both a science and an art and greatly depends on the experience of the general sales manager.

Like so much else in life, the budgeting process is interlinked with the self-interest of the decision-makers. A general sales managers, whose compensation is linked to achievement of sales goals, understandably wants the smallest reasonable goals the company will accept.

The general sales manager provides analysis and recommendations, but at the end of the process, the general manager is responsible for proposing next year's sales projections, which is another reason you must have full command of the facts, history, and projections that make up the revenue budget.

As the general manager, your compensation is dependent on achieving profit goals, so you are naturally motivated to increase sales while containing expenses. Your boss, the group or company head, is also motivated to achieve profit. If you work for a public company, you and your boss likely have stock options, a classic profit motivator.

The reality is more complex than just one year's profit number. The only way to increase sales year after year (thus raising long-term profit) is to also increase investment in the product, meaning you must find the best balance between the two. This sometimes means making investments that might actually hurt your bonus in a given year. Willingness to look at the long run is a key component of becoming a great general manager.

Forecasting

In addition to the annual budgeting process, companies understandably want monthly and quarterly updates on sales projections. As the general manager, you should expect thoughtful analysis from the general sales manager. You are also responsible for the forecast, so make sure you understand it and agree with the analysis before sending it in.

Political Advertising

The Supreme Court has ruled that political advertising by candidates is a form of political speech. That means a television station is not allowed to censor or change a certified candidate's advertising. Occasionally, a politician will produce a commercial that is outrageous or does not meet the standards a station would require a regular advertiser to meet. In those cases, free speech invariably trumps any content objections the station may have.

Certified candidates are also able to buy advertising at the lowest unit rate a station sells to other advertisers during a specific window of time. Lowest unit rates, availability of time periods, and other political advertising issues are complex and constantly changing. Stations always employ attorneys or outside legal firms with expertise in this area, but attorneys are not the last word. Every general manager should have an in-depth understanding of political rules.

Noncandidate political advertising is called issue advertising. Issue spots are subject to the same pricing and content rules as normal commercials. They have no right to lowest unit rate, which means a station can charge a higher rate than that paid by regular commercial clients.

Political advertising for state and national candidates is usually bought by one of the specialized political advertising agencies in Washington, DC. That makes a station's national sales manager the point person on most political ads. Be it the national manager or someone else you designate, each station should have someone on staff who is constantly being updated on the latest rules.

In addition to the rules regarding placement and content of political advertising, stations must also maintain a current database online with the FCC. Any member of the public can access the online database, so getting the details right is critical. Mistakes can result in massive fines.

There are two bottom-line rules when dealing with political advertising: The first is to know the current regulations and make sure you are in compliance. The second is to always get cash in advance.

Regulation

Both the Federal Trade Commission (FTC) and the Federal Communications Commission (FCC) regulate station sales practices. Some state regulations also apply. Rules can sometimes change quickly. Because you can't afford to get this wrong, broadcasting groups retain counsel to advise on current regulations. Make sure you are not only up-to-date but that you fully understand the rules. Failure to do so could not only be embarrassing but potentially cost you your job.

This book is not an appropriate forum to discuss every nuance of sales regulation. However, there is one rule that you must never forget, even for a moment. Any collusion between stations to fix prices or otherwise coordinate financial dealings is against the law. If discovered, you could face a federal felony prosecution. In my entire career, I've never seen that happen, but that is not to say it could not. Always be on your guard.

Competing television stations are not allowed to discuss inventory pricing, how much a station pays for programming, what inventory will be available for sale, or any other item that would appear to be collusion. A prosecutor could see what might seem to be an innocent conversation between two salespeople at competing stations as collusion.

Dealing with time buyers can be very frustrating, especially when they lie to you, so it is understandable why some salespeople might be tempted to talk with someone from another station. This is not just a bad idea; it could conceivably put both people in jail. At the very least, it would destroy a career. As the general manager, it is your job to set the standard, both vocally and by your own actions, that make it clear you will not condone any bending of the law.

General Sales Managers

One thing that has been constant over the years is the rise of general sales managers to general manager positions. There are a number of reasons for this, including the fact sales managers are used to large financial responsibility, know how to deal with the reality of strong or poor ratings, are often big-picture people, and, perhaps most importantly, know how to sell themselves.

Sales managers who want to become general managers are well advised to spend time learning news. This is best done by building a relationship with the news director. The more a sales manager knows about the product, the better candidate that manager is for higher responsibility.

The Secret Sales Weapon

Well-respected television sales trainer Jim Doyle is fond of saying, "Generals meet with generals." What Doyle means is that general managers have a unique opportunity to build relationships directly with the owners and heads of major clients.

Because we are so intimately involved with our stations, it's easy to forget that to most people, local television is a glamorous business. A call from a television station general manager to the head of a major business is usually well received, especially since the general manager is not calling to sell advertising.

Over the years, I've built relationships with a wide variety of major clients as well as ad agency heads. I've always made these relationships personal, not directly related to business, though I have, of course, talked about the station and why I'm so proud of the people who work there. What I can tell you is that almost without exception, these relationships have resulted in the clients spending more money on whatever station I was leading.

Here's how it works. The client tells people in his organization that WXXX's general manager is a friend. That information eventually filters down to the people making planning or buying decisions. It is only human nature for a buyer to not want to upset a friend of her boss.

None of this takes the place of personally calling on buyers—which is the appropriate place for a sales pitch about the station—but a relationship with the buyer's boss, or the actual client, is well worth the effort.

Sales and News

One of the things that often happens when a station is failing is that some part of the wall between sales and news is breached. As ratings drop, so does revenue, which puts pressure on the general manager to find new ways to add revenue. Once a story ends up on the news as part of an advertising deal, everything else goes downhill. I've seen commercials squeezed over end credits, commercial crawls during newscasts, anchors appearing in commercials, you name it. I once arrived at a station to find not only all of the above going on but also that every element of the newscast was sponsored.

I suppose mixing sales and news could have some self-justification if all this fixed the station's financial problems, but I've never seen that be the case. What usually happens is the buyers see all these things as "added value" to the schedule, meaning they don't actually pay much for them.

Here is why all those things are a bad idea. Sales influence in the news product destroys the credibility of your news product. The core financial value of a television station is based on viewer trust. If viewers feel a station's news product is being influenced by commercial interests, or any other outside forces for that matter, they will no longer trust the product. That means they will stop using that product, thus destroying the value of the station. It's just that simple.

I'm not saying there should be no relationship between sales and news. Quite the opposite. Ole Miss professor Dr. Deb Wenger and I wrote a book called *Managing Today's News Media: Audience First*, which makes the case for department heads being on the same brand page. But those relationships should be on a department head level.

Finally, integrity is a great sales tool. Clients want to be in an atmosphere they can trust. If other stations have questionable practices, your integrity becomes even more valuable.

Summary

Sales is a key area that determines the success or failure of a station. Investing the time it takes to learn the nuances of sales is well worth the investment. Building a strong local department means also building a foundation for the future.

Though old images linger, modern sales departments are professional and hardworking. Both managers and account executives are motivated to win. They are also well compensated.

Though there is a corollary between ratings and revenue, great sales departments produce higher revenue shares than their holding capacity would indicate. Selling less than ratings holding capacity is never acceptable.

Demographic ratings are the primary revenue currency. Some categories, such as women ages twenty-five through fifty-four, are far more valuable than others.

Building a business relationship with key advertising time buyers is a good investment of a general manager's time. This gives the general manager an opportunity to tell the station's story. Because time buyers are less well paid than salespeople, lunches at good restaurants and other perks, such as tickets to athletic events, are normal practices.

General managers who do not come from the sales ranks need to learn and fully understand the sales process. Many of the intricacies of sales, including projections and budgeting, require the general manager's involvement.

Because television sales inventory is a perishable product that has no value after its sell-by date, inventory must be properly priced. A station that is "sold out" is not properly monetizing inventory, nor is one that is only 70 percent sold. There are many excuses for being sold out, or for not correctly pricing, but none is acceptable.

Determining the amount of inventory before and during a newscast is an inexact science. In general, though, shorter breaks with fewer commercials help retain viewers.

Nielsen uses panels to estimate household and demographic ratings. Digital platforms have the advantage of exact audience measurement. Eventually, all media will have exact audience measurement.

Political advertising is highly regulated and requires both outside counsel and on-staff expertise.

Both the Federal Communications Commission and the Federal Trade Commission regulate television advertising. Any collusion between stations is a bad idea that can lead to federal charges.

Understanding the correct relationship between sales and news is critical to the long-term success of stations.

Key Takeaways

- General managers who do not come from sales need to invest time in learning the intricacies of the selling process.
- The relationship between ratings and revenue is variable based upon the skills of sales management. Selling beyond ratings holding capacity is a key metric for success.
- Many things, including positive business relationships with time buyers, affect the buying and selling process. Involvement of the general manager can make a difference.
- Traditional audience measurement is estimated, but digital platforms measure actual usage. At some point, all media measurement will be of actual usage.
- Television advertising is highly regulated. Understanding constantly changing rules is a boilerplate requirement for every general manager.
- Maintaining the integrity of a station's news department is critical to sales success.

11

PROGRAMMING

With so much of the major syndicated programming now being bought group-wide, it would be easy to think of programming as a low priority. That would be a mistake.

People, programming, and network payments are the three largest categories of expenses in most stations' budgets. Cost alone should make programming a high priority on any general manager's agenda. Just as important is the value of syndicated programming as a lead-in to news and other station programming. No single program stands alone. Each plays an interactive part with other functions of the station.

Dayparts

With the exception of morning news shows and a few soap operas, most daytime program periods are filled with syndicated shows that stations purchase.

The most important syndicated time period is the hour preceding a station's afternoon newscasts because some of that program's audience will flow into the newscasts. The days of megashows, like *Oprah*, that could move a station's newscast from last to first place are behind us, though one can never tell about the future. Up until the recession back in 2008, stations that carried *Oprah* paid license fees that were often equal to the total sales revenue in the program. Why buy a show that does not make money? Because of its value as a lead-in to local news.

Determining lead-in value is always dicey. It's not a matter of simply calculating audience flow, then assigning a dollar value. How much worse would a lower-priced program perform? How much better would a higher-priced show do? What effect does counterprogramming on other stations have? How much of the audience flow is due to the program, and how much is due to news loyalty? It's not an exact science, which is why you have to spend time understanding it.

Access programming, the time period between local news and prime time, is a completely different question. One rarely buys an access program because of flow into network programming. Access is all about profit, length of contracts, and counterprogramming on competing stations.

Daytime programming is far less important than news lead-in and access, but it still matters. Premiering a show in daytime, then letting it grow into something that might work as a news lead-in is an age-old strategy. The idea is to buy what could become a news lead-in or access show early at a good multiyear price. That's exactly how *Oprah* launched back during the mid-1980s. In between *Oprah's* launch and today, there have been at least fifty programs designed to replace *Oprah*. Most have failed. None of the few that have succeeded has come close to matching its unique success, but that does not mean anyone has stopped trying.

Pricing

There was a time when we bought shows for fixed prices, then played them in whatever time period the station thought made sense. Some stations even bought programs to put "on the shelf," meaning the station did not have a time period to air the show but wanted to make sure a competitor could not air it. Of course, that would not make economic sense today, though occasionally a station will end up with a program they have no place to play.

All program pricing these days is time-period specific. There may also be prenegotiated pricing should a daytime show become a hit and move to a more important time period. Back in the dark ages when I was a program director at the CBS affiliate in Washington, DC, we bought *Wheel of Fortune* for a pittance because no one thought it would work—including us. When the show became a hit, it cost us a fortune to renew it a few years later. Still, we enjoyed incredible profits during the initial contract period.

Barter Matters

When considering programming, one must also take barter into account. Virtually every Monday-through-Friday syndicated show, with rare exceptions, has a license fee plus barter. Barter means the syndicator keeps some of the program's commercial inventory to sell on the national barter market.

Barter is a bad thing for affiliates because it reduces the amount of commercial time a station has to sell. Unfortunately, barter is seen by the industry as just a fact of life since syndicators will not normally negotiate the amount of barter in any particular show. Unless a syndicator has the same number of barter spots on each station across the country, they can't sell that inventory in the national market. It is a dumb system because barter is sold at a fraction of its real worth. Both stations and syndicators would be better off doing away with barter and raising license fees instead. The odds of that are less than unlikely. Maybe it's too sensible.

If you want to understand the full impact of barter, look at your average unit rate in a time period and multiply that by the number of barter units in the same program. It can be a big number.

Weekend programming, the once-a-week shows that fill some of a station's nonnetwork programmed time periods, is almost exclusively barter, usually a fifty-fifty split. That means the program does not have a cash license fee, but you only get 50 percent of the commercial inventory. It's tough to sell advertising for a premium rate during an odd half hour on Saturday late night or Sunday afternoon, so an all-barter agreement can make sense in this kind of scenario. Even so, I would still rather have a cash deal.

Off-network sitcoms in their initial syndicated season also contain barter, but older evergreen shows, like *Andy Griffith,* normally do not. Evergreen (meaning the program continues to have value years after production ends) shows are straight cash, as are most movie packages. Regular affiliates rarely run movies anymore. There are just not many appropriate time periods. Affiliation contracts with networks also make it difficult to find regular time periods for programming longer than one hour.

On very rare occasions during high-demand times, a station will preempt an evening of prime time to run a syndicated movie or other nonnetwork program. This is done in order to increase the amount of prime-time inventory the station can sell that evening. This is called a make-good theater. Network contracts have pretty well done away with make-good theaters, but they still occasionally occur.

Paid Programming

From the earliest days of television, some advertising clients have preferred to buy thirty-minute programs for their products. Over the years, the range of products and services has greatly increased, but all share the same business model: selling consumer goods or services directly to the consumer. Some clients do the same thing using spot inventory. This is called direct response or DR for short.

Paid religious programming is a subcategory, which can sometimes be very lucrative.

Every television station carries some level of paid programming. Why? Because it's easier than trying to sell spots in an odd time period. Some stations fill weekend afternoons with paid, but others prefer to limit paid because they believe it has a negative effect on their brands.

Group Deals

Most large syndication deals are now done on the corporate level. Even though you might not be actually negotiating with syndicators to buy programming, you still need to make your voice heard at corporate. Every market is different. Part of your responsibility as a general manager is to understand your market and know what kind of programming fits your station and your community. That means taking the time to meet with the various syndicators who call on you. It can also mean a nice lunch. An important goal of any syndicator worth her salt is to put a general manager's name on her expense report.

Negotiation

Not all programming is bought by corporate, so knowing everything available is also important. Your programming manager should be keeping a full competitive list of every station and every syndicated program airing in the market, including pricing, terms, and contract dates for each individual show. Let me be clear. You cannot get this information directly from competing stations. You could be accused of colluding with your competitors, a serious crime. The best source of pricing is the syndicators themselves.

Syndicators are salespeople, so they will do their best to generate competitive interest in a program among all stations in a market. Expect them to stretch the truth from time to time. You, on the other hand, want a reputation for always being straightforward, so never mislead anyone. This is a business of reputations and long memories. It is critical that whatever you say can be taken to the bank. That does not mean revealing everything you know. Information is a key negotiating tool.

Good syndicators do their homework and come to the table with a full understanding of every station's program schedule, pricing, competitive situation, and programming needs. It is your responsibility to be equally well informed. The syndicator wants to close a sale and do it at the highest possible price. Your job is to understand the full landscape, including what other stations are paying for programs, and then make the best possible decision for your station. You can't blame a syndicator for trying to shoehorn a show into your schedule that makes no sense for the station, so be prepared to give each syndicator a full hearing even when you know it is highly unlikely you will buy their product. The same syndicator may have just the show you need next time.

If you have an important programming decision to make, be sure to include the general sales manager and, if appropriate, the news director in the process. Their opinions can be very helpful, along, of course, with your programming manager. One of the things you do not want to do is present the sales department with a new program to sell that they don't believe in. That sometimes happens because of group deals, but avoid it when you can. A sales department's enthusiasm for a product matters.

Even though you may not have full control of purchases, syndicated programming is a critical component of a station's success. It is worth spending the time and effort to fully understand it, therefore enabling you to make the best decisions possible.

Local Programming

Local television has a great history of program development. Shows like *Phil Donahue, Oprah*, and *Live with Kelly and Ryan* all began as local shows. The success of those programs has caused most of the larger groups to get into the programming business, usually beginning at the station level. Success in the world of syndication is a rare thing, so the odds of a local program being successful, much less going national, are quite long. Even though the odds are stacked against a company, the financial reward for success can be staggering, so companies continue to make the investment in program development.

As for truly local programming, some of the larger stations still have actual programming departments that produce local shows, but that has become rare. A station's news department now produces most local programming.

Children's Programming

Most children's programming is provided and scheduled by a station's network, but that does not mean you can afford to ignore this crucial area. FCC fines for failure to follow children's programming rules can be severe, even draconian. These rules govern everything about children's programming, from the amount of programming that must be aired to what time periods are required, how programs can be preempted, how many commercials can run within a program, what the content of those commercials are, even how announcements of upcoming changes are made. These and many other nuances have to be gotten right.

Every station has someone, usually the program director (or coordinator) who is responsible for knowing the rules and making sure they are followed to the letter. As the general manager, you also must have a working knowledge of the rules. Failure in this area can be a career killer. No manager wants to be in the position of explaining a publicly embarrassing FCC fine to his or her company.

Relationship with Corporate

Every broadcast group of any size has someone in charge of programming. The ability to negotiate a group of stations at one time gives the corporate program manager leverage with syndicators. The final price is dependent on the number of markets, time periods, and other factors, all of which have to be negotiated. Once a deal has been completed, corporate managers then assign a specific price to each station.

Group programming decisions are not made in a vacuum. A corporate program manager usually works closely with general managers to make sure there is input from each local station. This relationship can work very well, but it is up to you, the general manager, to make sure the relationship is developed. Not doing so can result in some nasty surprises, such as a much higher allocation fee than you had expected.

Some companies, especially the mega ones, think in terms of a national footprint, which means local stations have less of a voice in program purchase decisions. Even in those cases, some decisions are still made locally. Moreover, just because a company has a group-wide deal, that does not mean a particular program runs in the same time period on each station.

Program Directors

Prior to the era of large companies and the rise of local news as a station's most important product, program directors were important department heads with responsibility for syndicated and local programming, production staff, and many other areas.

As station groups grew and group program managers gained power, the definition of program director on the local level changed. Instead of a major department head, the person in charge of programming became more of a scheduler and network programming coordinator with miscellaneous other duties, such as overseeing children's programming regulations and being responsible for closed captioning. Many people in the programming job today have a lesser title, such as program coordinator. It is also common for programming to be combined with another job, such as research director.

Whatever title your programming person has, his or her function is still important, even though general managers now make most of the decisions formerly made by program directors. No matter how your station is organized, you must have a quality person who is detail oriented overseeing this critical area.

Information and Attitude

In negotiating your way through the world of syndication, your most important tools are information and attitude. Information gives you a clear picture of options, costs, and potential returns. Attitude means you make decisions logically and methodically. Everyone who has spent time in a programming job has stories of stations that paid too much or bought the wrong show because they got caught up in the competition to do a deal. Don't let that be you. Making a decision on parameters prior to the negotiation, then sticking with those parameters, will serve you well.

Also, never buy a program just because you like it. Chances are you are not a member of the target audience. If a program is targeted at stay-at-home moms, find out what stay-at-home moms think. You liking a program is the first step, but I could probably write a whole chapter on general managers I have known who've made the fatal programming mistake of buying a show they liked without having any idea how the target group felt.

Summary

Syndicated programming is an important part of any station's schedule. Although group program managers now buy most programming, general managers still play an important role.

The most valuable syndicated daypart is the hour before afternoon news begins. Audience flow from the syndicated program to a station's local newscast can play an important part in news ratings. Prime access, the period between local news and the start of prime time, is the second most important part. Access programming does not affect news lead-ins, so it is chosen based on potential profitability.

It is essential that general managers understand the entire syndicated makeup of a market, including what other television stations pay. The best source for that information is the syndicators themselves. Never discuss syndication with another television station.

Barter is an important component of a program's profitability because it reduces available inventory. Some once-a-week programs in minor time periods are sold on a barter basis. In those cases, barter can make more sense than a license fee.

Children's programming is an important area because failure to follow federal rules exactly can result in a large and embarrassing fine. Rules constantly change, so someone in your organization must be fully up to speed at all times. Ultimately, you are responsible.

Negotiation is a matter of understanding the entire landscape, including current pricing across the market, then determining parameters prior to beginning the discussion. Stations that have not locked in parameters can be stampeded into a bad deal. Even when a corporate program manager buys a program, you still must understand the effect on your station so that you can speak up before a deal is completed.

Key Takeaways

- Understanding the entire syndicated makeup of your market, including pricing, is an essential part of your job.
- Most big deals are now done by corporate program managers, but stations must still give input. Otherwise, you can end up with a program or cost allocation you do not like.
- Children's programming is a very big deal because of the potential for violating federal regulations. Fines and embarrassment are both severe.
- Programming is often the second-highest expense category in any station, behind people, so making the best decisions, both on pricing and schedule, is critical.
- Never buy a program just because you like it. Find out how the target audience feels.

12

Engineering

Most new general managers have almost no background in the technical side of media, so when it comes to engineering, they are tempted to stay completely big picture, leaving all the details to their chief engineer. This has never been a good idea, even back in the days when technology was relatively simple.

Technology is now advancing so fast—especially with the introduction of artificial intelligence, big data, and virtual reality—that a general manager needs to have a working understanding of not only technology but also workflow. I'm not suggesting you know exactly what makes things work, but you do need to know why a project is worth spending a million dollars on.

For instance, field cameras equipped with cell cards were a game changer because they allowed stations to feed all images to the cloud live, making everything available instantly on every platform. That instantaneous, unedited capability allowed mobile and other digital platforms to provide unique live coverage separate from what a viewer might see on television.

Converting every field camera to upload live to the cloud sounds like a no-brainer. But what about the cameras that will be replaced? Have they reached their useful life? What about the operating cost of multiple cell phone cards all transmitting at once? What about other operational and equipment priorities? A station can never buy everything it wants, so prioritizing is a critical decision that cannot simply be left to the chief engineer.

If the technical area is new to you, the best way to learn is to ask questions. "Tell that to me in English" is a time-honored general manager's line when talking to chief engineers. Don't be afraid to show your lack of knowledge. No one expects you to have a background in video flow or equipment design.

The chief engineer is your best source for technical information but not necessarily workflows or the technical priorities of other departments. Understanding those operational issues means you must also be able to have an intelligent conversation with other department heads, particularly the news director. Again, do not be afraid to ask questions. News departments have incredible tools that are not hard to understand once you really get into them. For instance, a producer used to just put a show together. Today, that same producer is calling up graphics, editing video, searching multiple databases, and a host of other functions. Understanding how a producer's job works is critical when you make upgrade decisions.

It is also not unusual for chief engineers and news directors to have different priorities. You are the referee.

None of this is as difficult as you might think. The key is to see how everything fits into the overall picture.

Engineering Logic

I've known a lot of chief engineers. Some are stereotypical nerds, but most these days are not. Television has moved from fairly straightforward equipment-based systems to IP-based systems. Engineering departments still own soldering irons, but rarely does anyone actually fix something. They are more likely to replace a bad card or send a part back to the factory.

This switch to computer-based systems has forced chief engineers to broaden their horizons, which is good for you. Any solid chief engineer can tell you the station's technical priorities and goals for the next few years. You may or may not agree with those priorities, but the discussion starts with the chief's needs analysis and long-range plan to fill those needs.

The ability to think logically is the hallmark of every strong chief. Unfortunately, not everything in media fits within the logical world the average chief engineer wants to live in. This sometimes creates friction with other department heads who only care about their needs. Part of your job is to help the other department realize that input from a logically thinking engineer can help them because he or she sometimes sees things everyone else overlooks. Once the chief understands why a department head wants to do a particular thing, he or she can look for the best technical solution.

Relationship with News

If chief engineers think logically, news directors can be prone to throwing logic out the window. They are about solving the problem at hand. What happens tomorrow is tomorrow's problem. Chief engineers plan for the long term. News directors are pretty much locked into today. Chief engineers want equipment to be used as designed. News directors want equipment to do exactly what they need it to do at any given moment. When a piece of equipment fails, a chief engineer wants to find out why. News directors want it fixed immediately, even if that means taping it up.

Because they see the world so differently, some level of conflict between chief engineers and news directors is a given.

As the general manager, your job is to build a relationship between two people who may not completely trust each other. Without your intervention, a negative relationship can lead to major problems. Any kind of feud between department heads saps energy, kills creativity, and destroys atmosphere. Chief engineers and news directors do not start out with the intention of being at odds, but the natural differences in how they see the world usually lead to some form of tension.

The best way to build a relationship between a news director and a chief engineer is to deal with it head-on. Reaching station goals will not be possible unless these two department heads work together. Each one needs to understand the kind of pressures the other is under. Each can and should help each other. Each one also needs to understand the other also wants to win.

The daily operations meeting I mentioned in a previous chapter can be an important tool. By putting these people together each day, you are in a position to help solve small issues before they become big ones. Your presence creates a different dynamic that gives you a measure of control.

However you choose to deal with it, the natural conflict between engineering and news is a real thing that requires your involvement.

Capital Expense

Every station has two kinds of budgets: the operating budget and the capital budget. The point person for the capital budget is usually the chief engineer.

Capital expenses are large items, such as buildings and equipment, that are designed to function over several years. Because of their multiyear life-spans, the IRS does not allow the full cost of these items to be deducted in the year they are purchased. Instead, these costs are spread over a number of years. This is called depreciation, meaning a piece of equipment becomes steadily less valuable each year over its useful life. It depreciates in value.

The actual process is far more complicated. Every company

has their own rules and policies, which can vary widely. Plus, there are many other aspects to the capital process, so you need to have a full understanding of how it all works. This begins with the chief engineer explaining the current state of the operation, what needs to be currently replaced, and what investments need to be made for the future and why. This is not a one-way conversation. You need to be able to question, challenge, and make suggestions.

Most companies have a capital budget process that is not only separate from the operating budget but often comes at a different time of year. Because the capital process emphasizes long-term needs and costs, it can be easy to forget these purchases will also have an effect on your operating profit, so make sure you fully understand what that $1 million piece of equipment means to operating expense and the profit line.

Sometimes a review of operating expenses will show that new piece of technology you want to buy might not be worth the total cost to your operation.

Engineering Role in Public Emergencies

One way to think of television stations is as independent units connected to a network signal but otherwise fully self-contained. Stations maintain their own transmitters, towers, generators, and diesel fuel storage, meaning they have the ability to function as stand-alone units during natural disasters, such as hurricanes, or in the event of a national emergency. The ability to stay on the air during natural or man-made disasters makes local television and radio essential public services.

Unlike any other media, network-affiliated television stations have the resources to function as local information hubs, providing lifesaving information to the communities they serve. This ability to serve a local community in times of crisis is what makes television different from cable, satellite, OTT, and other services. The role of first responder is a critical one for every local station. Without properly thought-out, maintained, and updated equipment and facilities, television could not serve this role.

A station's chief engineer must know in advance how the station will operate during an extended emergency. Can the entire plant operate off generators? How long will the supply of diesel fuel last, and how will it be replenished? What happens if the studios suffer a catastrophe and are unusable? What is the backup plan for an emergency facility? What happens if the tower goes down? Answers to these and other critical questions must be part of a station's emergency plan.

Future of Technology

When I began working in television, it took five people to switch a station break, which included a live booth announcer. During the film era, a news crew often consisted of four people: reporter, photographer, audio person, film loader / lighting person. During the mid-1970s, many in our industry believed videotape would never replace film. When videotape was finally accepted, the idea of doing a news story with only a reporter and photographer was considered cheap and unworkable.

My point is that our business has always changed and will continue to do so. Technology will continue to replace people while growing capabilities at the same time. The debate between technological advancement and changes that are done just to save money will also continue. There will be both mistakes and bold, logical moves. Your job as the general manager is not just to employ experts or depend on your company for guidance but to have a real understanding of equipment and operations so that you can play a part in creating the future.

You do not have to become an expert in engineering to lead your station into the future, but you must have enough knowledge to understand how the big picture and the pieces work together.

Summary

A new general manager without a background in the technical side of media needs to take the time to learn. The best source of information is usually the chief engineer.

No station can afford to buy everything it might want, so the general manager must be prepared to prioritize needs. This includes the ability to look at the operational costs of technical equipment. Both the chief engineer and the news director will offer input, but responsibility for final decisions rests with the general manager.

Engineers and news directors are often at odds because they view the world from different perspectives. Engineers think logically and long-term. News directors must solve immediate problems. The best way to foster an effective relationship is for the general manager to be involved on a daily basis.

The capital expense budget is separate from a station's operating budget, but it is no less important. It still affects a station's profit.

Television stations are uniquely situated to serve their local communities during natural or man-made disasters. Every station should have a plan to maintain technical operations, no matter the public emergency.

Technology will continue to change rapidly. General managers should understand enough about technology that they can lead change.

Key Takeaways

- Every general manager must have a working knowledge of technology. Simply leaving decisions up to the chief engineer is not acceptable.
- Capital costs are an important expense item. Therefore, the general manager must be able to evaluate each potential purchase, including operational costs.
- Chief engineers and news directors see the world differently. Positive working relationships require involvement of the general manager.
- Technology will continue to change. General managers must be prepared to lead that change as part of the big picture.

13

Business Office

The business manager is your first line of defense in preventing fraud, controlling expenses, and ensuring corporate policies are followed. The best business managers are strong enough to hold their own with other department heads, making news directors and sales managers toe the line when costs start to get out of control.

Because the business manager has access to all contracts and salaries, discretion and confidentiality are essential. This access to information makes the business manager the one person you can talk to about sensitive financial matters.

As stations have found ways to reduce expenses, many business managers have also taken on the employee relations role with varying success. I've been fortunate enough to have managers whose personalities help them empathize with employees, but I also know of more than one case where a hard-nosed business manager should be the last person dealing with people's problems.

Above all, a business manager must be trustworthy. I've said to more than one, "Your job is to keep me out of jail. That means holding everyone accountable—even me."

Of all the things a business manager does, the most significant is preparing the annual operating budget. You are ultimately responsible for the budget, but the business manager does the detail work.

Budgeting Process

Your station's budget is the financial tool that supports implementation of your strategic plan. A strategic plan without proper allocation of resources is a hollow instrument, incapable of success. Because of this, the budgeting process always begins with the strategic plan, not the other way around. That means you cannot simply leave the budget to the business manager. Even though you are not doing the detail work, you still must guide the process strategically and fully understand every detail.

The budget's ultimate goal is to support the strategic plan, but the starting point is the previous year's actual revenue, expense, and profit. The core nature of any business is profit, so next year's profit will always be judged by the current year and previous years. Every company expects reasonable profit growth—or in some instances, unreasonable—but that is something you cannot control. If profit expectations are unreasonable, you need to logically point out why, but the final decision will not be yours. If you find yourself fundamentally not aligned with your company's expectations, then you need to consider working for another company.

The cyclical nature of political advertising and the Olympics means the opportunity for profit is materially greater in even years than odd ones. For this reason, most companies compare both the current year and the past year when judging the next year's profit potential. This even-odd-year look interjects reasonableness into the process, especially in the case of public companies that are reporting to shareholders.

Because they have the advantage of looking at historic norms, most companies issue financial expectations to stations before the budgeting process begins. This expression is usually in percentage growth rather than specific dollars. Profit, of course, varies from station to station, but corporate benchmarks are the yardstick each one uses.

Revenue

For most of its history, television revenue came almost exclusively from spot sales supported by cash payments from networks, a system called network comp. Up until it was phased out in the late 1990s, network comp made up a significant portion of some smaller stations' profits.

In theory, network comp was a station's share of network advertising spot sales. When networks began to change hands in the 1980s, more than one new owner wanted to end comp payments. They believed the revenue stations gained from local spots in prime-time programming and major sports events was more than fair payment. Some were bold enough to suggest stations should be paying the networks, not the other way around. By the early 2000s, network comp was pretty much gone, with both networks and local stations responsible for their own revenue.

The game changer in the financial relationship between networks and affiliated stations was retransmission consent. When stations began to receive significant financial payments from cable and satellite companies, networks made the not unreasonable case that some of that revenue was the result of highly viewed network programming. Thus, reverse comp came into existence. It's fair to say that today's reverse comp payments are significantly larger than the ones made by networks back in the compensation days.

Even after the network collects a percentage of retransmission fees, the total retransmission dollars left at the average station are still greater than network comp payments ever approached. In fact, the affiliated station model probably would no longer work without retransmission consent payments. Mobile and web revenue also continue to grow, as does D-2 network advertising, so traditional national and local spot sales, while still the bulk of a station's revenue, no longer carry the revenue burden alone.

Station spot revenue is divided into two streams: national and local. As we discussed in another chapter, national advertising, buffeted by the explosion of internet and mobile advertising revenue, continues to be in long decline. Local, on the other hand, is a growth opportunity, not so much from traditional agency business as from direct sales to local merchants.

Taking all this into account, a revenue budget will account for each revenue stream independently: local, national, retransmission, web sales, and multiplexed D2 networks, usually in that order of importance. Local is first because it is the stream a station has the most control over.

Other items in the revenue section include anything from tower rental to use fees charged to others. Many of these are categorized simply as "other revenue."

The general sales manager is the key player in creating the station's revenue plan, but that does not let the general manager off the hook. The general manager, not the GSM, submits the station budget to corporate. Revenue is ultimately the general manager's responsibility.

Expense

Budgeting expenses is much more complex. Most stations base the next year's budget on current expenses, which is a reasonable expectation but with a downside. The temptation is to simply add or subtract money from the previous year's actuals rather than to think the budget through.

The proper way to do an expense budget is to zero base assumptions. That means each expense should be approached with the following questions: Does this expenditure support the station's strategic plan? Is this the best way to invest? Is this expense really necessary? Could this money be better spent in another area?

Every station has sacred cow expenses that are not really needed. If you decide to keep those in the budget, make sure you know exactly what they are and the order of priority you will cut them if the year goes bad. Of course, some expenses are simply boilerplate and can't be changed, but that is no excuse for not fully considering every other cost.

The expense process usually begins with each department head creating a proposed budget. This will inevitably contain some blue-sky expenses, but that's OK. You want the department heads to think big. What is not OK is simply adding a percentage increase to each line. The same goes with salaries. Not every employee contributes to the same degree, so not every employee should receive the same percentage raise. Remember too that highly compensated employees can't be judged just on percentages. You also have to consider value and fairness all the way around. Companies usually dictate an overall percentage in total salary growth they expect for the coming year, but how that percentage is distributed requires hard work on the department head's part.

After the department head finishes, the business manager sits down with the department head to go through the budget line by line, suggesting changes. This forces the department head to be focused and realistic.

Once the business manager and department head are aligned, they go through the numbers line by line with the general manager. This is the GM's opportunity to question and adjust each expense. This part of the process is especially critical because the GM will be presenting the final budget to corporate, where questioning will likely be intense.

Profit

Revenue minus expense results in profit, but actually determining profit is much more complex. The initial roll-up may show an unreasonably small profit. If that happens, either revenue must be raised or expenses decreased. Usually, it is a combination of both.

Profit matters. Stations that are marginally profitable have difficulty justifying investment. Staff size is affected. Extras go away. Bad things in general happen. High-profit stations are well positioned to invest in new initiatives and new ideas. Profit is not just an exercise; it affects everything a station does.

At the end of the process, if the submitted budget does not meet corporate expectations, revenue and/or expense will be changed by the company.

In my thirty-plus years of running stations, I never submitted a budget I could not fully justify. I always expected the budget to be approved as submitted, not that it actually worked out that way. If a department head request was over the top or obviously unreasonable, I didn't put it in. Not everyone agrees with this philosophy, believing they should put everything they could possibly want in a budget and then let the corporate people cut it. The problem with that approach is that once corporate realizes they have been given an unrealistic budget, which takes about two seconds, they take control of the process. You lose control of what stays and what goes. That's a very bad thing. If I'm responsible for achieving a budget, I want to control the process. Otherwise, I could lose important initiatives in the general cutting.

If you know changes will happen, it is much better to make them yourself.

Budget Implementation

Like your strategic plan, your budget is a living tool that affects your station's daily operation. Good general managers review revenue every day and expenses at the end of every month. They also expect department heads and the business manager to let them know of unexpected costs or savings as soon as they come up.

Let's say you are halfway through the year and revenue is not meeting expectations. Because you understand the budget, you already know where to decrease spending. I've found it helpful to maintain tight control of expenses for the first quarter of each year. This allows you to build a reserve should sales not be as strong as expected.

If you find the need to reduce expenses, it's important that you have a specific plan. Can certain personnel hires be delayed? What nonessential expenses can be eliminated? What things can be put off until business is better? The best way to determine these things is by the general manager and business manager working together, but if you are doing your jobs, both of you know the answers well in advance.

One note on expense reductions. Be smart enough to know what can be saved and what would be stupid to save. Repaving the parking lot might be able to wait, but not fixing a safety issue or repairing a broken satellite truck would be dumb.

Remember that the budget is a living document that constantly changes. I'd love to be smart enough to produce a budget that matches actual revenue, expense, and profit at the end of the year. That will never happen. All three elements are constantly in play. Your job is to make sure you are in control of the budget. Otherwise, it will control you.

Summary

A budget is the financial instrument that supports a station's strategic plan.

Business managers must be absolutely trustworthy, reliable, and accurate. Nothing less is acceptable.

Because he or she is the only person other than the general manager that has access to all financial information, the business manager also acts as a confidential advisor.

The revenue process is initially controlled by the general sales manager, but the general manager is ultimately responsible. Local spot sales are the largest component of revenue, followed by national spot sales and retransmission revenue.

Expense budgets are proposed by department heads, vetted by the business manager, and approved by the general manager. Should revenue not achieve budget, the business and general manager both know in advance what expense areas will be reduced. This has to be done smartly, since some savings would be unwise.

General managers who submit unrealistic budgets to corporate risk losing control of the process, making corporate responsible for which expense items are approved and which are denied. Giving control to corporate is a bad idea. Make the hard decisions yourself.

Implementing a budget is a daily process that constantly changes. That makes the budget a living document requiring regular attention.

Key Takeaways

- **The budgeting process begins with the station's strategic plan.**
- **The business manager must be absolutely reliable, capable of keeping information confidential, and able to advise the general manager about confidential financial matters.**

- Television stations have multiple revenue streams, but the one most in a station's control is local spot sales.
- Great general managers control the budgeting process, "owning" their budgets.
- Budgets are living documents that constantly change during implementation.

14

HUMAN RESOURCES

Unfortunately, the reality of today's business is that most stations no longer have a dedicated human resources manager. This does not mean employee relations are any less important today than in the past. It does mean general managers must now be more involved in this area.

No matter what size station you run, people are your greatest asset, your largest expense, and your biggest potential liability.

To understand the real cost of personnel, you need to also add Social Security, health care, 401(k) contributions, and the costs of all other benefits. From a financial point of view alone, every single person is expensive, so making sure each one is reaching his or her full potential is incredibly important.

If people are your most important asset, then hiring is obviously a critical function. Hiring the wrong person, something I've been guilty of more than once, is time consuming, draining, and expensive. So the human resources process begins with hiring. Clearly defining each position and determining exactly what skills are needed before posting a job are always worth the effort.

I wish hiring were an exact science, but it is not. All of us make hiring mistakes from time to time, so anything that increases odds of success is worth the effort. There are three essential components to the hiring process that can help you ultimately make great hires.

Qualifications

Résumés only tell part of a story. You need to dig deep into a person's job knowledge. I used to work with a news director in a good-sized market who gave potential reporter candidates a civics test. These were experienced people, not college kids. I was surprised how often candidates missed fairly simply questions. Performance and appearance are such important criteria in on-air talent that it can be easy to sometimes hire people who are all show and no substance.

Sales is another area fraught with potholes. Great personality and aggressiveness can sometimes mask poor work habits or a lack of interest in detail. Sales managers can be the first to fall for a personality that masks trouble. As the GM, you can serve as a great second opinion.

Track Record

When looking at a résumé, it is great to see a natural progression of advancement. Not seeing that can be a big red flag. A history of short stays in jobs is another red flag. Ask about each one in detail.

Who are the references on the résumé? Are they professionals? Are they supervisors or peers who will naturally say good things?

Look for anything on a résumé that seems odd or out of place. Remember, the applicant prepared the document, so it is their most impressive version of events. Any mistakes or errors are a bad sign. Ask questions in detail.

Never treat a résumé as a definitive document. It is a place to start.

Background Research

Driver's license checks and criminal background searches are unfortunately a good idea when hiring someone from outside your company. This is the last step before actually making an offer, so by this time, you are heavily invested in the person and anything that looks wrong will be a big disappointment. It is important to be fair. If something turns up that causes you to reconsider, give the candidate a chance to explain.

Hiring Someone Else's Problem

I'm sorry to say that some current employers will give a poor employee a glowing reference in the hope you will solve his or her problem. I've seen this happen more than once within the same company. Unless the recommender is a friend you trust, make sure you talk to multiple people.

What Does Your Gut Say?

Gut is a real thing. It is a summary of all your past experiences functioning on an unconscious level. If your gut is giving you alarms, listen to it. Conversely, if you immediately bond with the candidate, make sure you also follow through checking the person out. The world is full of poor hires by employers who followed their gut and nothing else.

If you find yourself falling in love with a candidate's personality, make sure he or she also interviews with other people at the station.

Above all, never take anything at face value.

Diversity

When Al Neuharth was running Gannett, he used to say that a media company's workforce should look like the people in the communities they served. Otherwise, it would be impossible to properly understand the needs and interests of users. Al was a smart man.

At its heart, diversity is about bringing a wide range of thoughts, backgrounds, and attitudes to the table. Not doing so means we run the risk of living in an echo chamber. Everyone in a company needs to be on the same page, but you can only be sure that is the proper page if you have looked at all options.

Finding minority candidates can sometimes be a challenge, so make sure you are constantly keeping an eye out for outstanding people. Great employees, no matter their background, will always be in demand, so the best time to recruit is before you have an opening.

FCC Record Keeping

The courts have ruled that the FCC cannot set required guidelines for hiring, but they can encourage recruitment of minorities by requiring extensive record keeping of community outreach. Like all other FCC rules, it is important you have a firsthand understanding of what must be achieved. Make sure you stay up-to-date on the current rules.

Performance Appraisals

Every company has its own systems and methods of doing performance appraisals. No matter what form this takes in your company, know this: if an employee is surprised by his or her annual review, you have not done your job.

People reporting to you need regular feedback from you, not just an annual conversation.

Every one of us needs to know if we are meeting expectations. Nothing is quite so bad as believing things are going well when they are not. Your job as a manager is to make sure each person who reports to you always knows where they stand. Without this knowledge, the person has no reason to take corrective action.

Cowards

Have you ever worked for a coward? I have. In fact, I have been one.

My first supervisory position was production manager at a medium-market NBC affiliate. One of our camera operators, whom we will call Joe, was terrible at his job. All the directors complained about Joe, but I kept putting off dealing with him. At the time, I thought it was because I didn't want to hurt his feelings, but I know now it was because I couldn't bring myself to tell Joe that he was incompetent.

Under pressure from the directors to do something, I finally called Joe into my office, then hemmed and hawed about the job he was doing. Joe asked for specifics, and I avoided the question, suggesting he talk with the directors.

Over the following weeks, Joe's performance did not improve. I was now getting pressure from the station manager, who said Joe had to go. I finally called Joe in and said we were laying him off.

"Why?" he asked.

"We just don't need you right now," was my cowardly answer.

During the following year, every time we had an opening for a camera operator, Joe would apply. I never hired him back and never told him the truth. I was too embarrassed to come clean.

Looking back, I had done the worst possible thing to an employee. Had I told Joe the truth—that running a camera was not his skill set—and given him the specific reasons he had asked for before being laid off, he might have been able to improve and save his job. Instead, he never understood, so he kept thinking he would get his job back.

As the years passed and the enormity of what I had done became clear, I resolved to never do anything like that to a person again. One of the most important things you can do for any employee is to tell the hard truths.

Terminations

People do not sue because you took their job away. They sue because you disrespected them.

That sounds simple, but it is true. To actually sue you, a person must be highly motivated. Any good lawyer will explain that suing an employer is a long and complex process that drains all parties involved. It can take years for a successful plaintiff to actually get a judgment, then even more years while the judgment is appealed. The process takes so long and is so overwhelming, it often puts a person's life on hold. Even then, there is no guarantee of collecting. So why would anyone ever sue? Because they feel so morally and righteously offended, they are willing to do whatever it takes to strike back.

Not only are lawsuits draining, they are expensive and embarrassing. You cannot control whether a person chooses to sue or not, but you can control the process leading up to termination in such a way that actually following through with a lawsuit is unlikely. That means always maintaining the moral high ground. Never let it get personal. Never do anything that is disrespectful.

I am not saying you can prevent people from getting angry about losing their jobs. Of course they will be angry. They will be devastated. Losing a job is a terrible thing. But to be maintained over time, anger must be combined with a deep and personal sense of unfairness and mistreatment. I call this being disrespected. By taking the time to make sure the employee sees you are trying to be fair and that, from your perspective, it is not personal, you make it far more likely the person will eventually move on with his or her life.

Let's take a look at the termination process and discuss some of the keys to success.

Why does someone lose a job? Usually it is because a person is in a job that does not fit his or her skill set and / or temperament. Some people lose their jobs because they are lazy or incompetent, but usually the root cause is a wrong fit for their skill set.

The first thing to understand about a termination is that your mind-set needs to be in the right place. You are doing what is best for both the company and the person. The decision to terminate came after the person was given every opportunity to improve.

Think of it this way. Every day a person spends in the wrong job is a day lost he could have invested in a job he was good at. When used properly and honestly, this is a powerful argument that can help a person in a poor fit exit the company and move on with his life.

Assuming you are doing a good job of managing, meaning you have properly laid out goals, prioritized them, provided necessary support, and provided regular honest feedback, the first step in separation is the formal job review.

As I indicated earlier, a formal review should not contain information the employee has never heard before. It should formalize the things that have already been discussed over time. It is important to depersonalize this process, concentrating on results that need to be achieved, not the motivations of the employee. This is a time to deal in facts, not personalities. Did the job get done? Why not? What needs to be done in the future?

Because this is a negative review, you are dealing with an uptight employee under great pressure. Your goal is to help the person turn things around, not termination. But if it is clear there may be a skill set issue, this can be a good time to first broach the subject not as an accusation but as a possible reason.

As part of the review, you need to present some kind of performance improvement plan that lays out specific expectations, a timetable, and the kind of support you plan to give the employee. A good plan provides regular feedback during the process. Feedback does two things. First, it gives the employee the best possible opportunity to succeed. Second, if the employee is not making progress, that fact will be evident to both of you. It is not unusual when this happens for the employee to solve your problem by quitting.

Let's fast-forward now over several months. You have laid out clear expectations and specific metrics that need to be achieved. Throughout this time, you have continued to concentrate on the job goals, trying to avoid accusations. Instead of saying "You did not do the job," say, "The job did not get done." Remember, the employee is an active participant in this process. He knows he did not get the job done; you are merely noting that a goal was not achieved.

If you go through this process in a reasonable and clear manner, it will become clear to the employee that you are trying to be fair. If you then move to termination, concentrate on job fit and the person's future. You have a responsibility to help the employee move on with his or her life. If you can give honest advice about what you think the person will be good at, do so. Don't mislead.

Don't tell an employee how badly you feel or how hard this is on you. You are not the one losing your job.

One of the things I always tell a person during a termination is that he or she should seek the advice of a professional attorney who deals with employment matters. That person will charge a fee but also give good advice.

Different companies have different policies, but I personally detest walking people out the door, then sending their personal belongings in a box. Far better to let them walk out on their own.

Offering to have someone meet them after hours or on Saturday morning so they can get their things also shows respect.

Let's assume now the person contacts an attorney for advice. A good attorney will hear the person's story and, if the attorney believes the case might have merit, ask the employer for a copy of his or her client's personnel file.

The personnel file is the single most critical factor in whether or not a lawsuit is filed. If you have done your job properly, it will lay out in detail your case for reasonable termination. If not, the attorney may smell money.

I have a rule of never personally talking to a plaintiff's attorney other than to refer them to our appropriate company attorney. You gain nothing by talking with someone else's lawyer. At this point, put the ball in your lawyer's court.

Most attorneys who actually take an employment case work on a percentage of the final settlement or judgment, if any. Time is money, so no attorney will sue unless he or she feels the case is strong. Most will make a phone call or write a letter asking for money, but actually taking the case to trial is a very big and expensive deal. No lawyer working on a percentage of a settlement will take a case to trial unless he or she feels confident of winning. If you have done your job creating a detailed personnel file and you have been careful to respect the employee, you can make a plaintiff's attorney think twice before going to court. You can often stop the process in its tracks.

Even when you are fully in the right, there are times when you will be willing to make a small settlement just to put the matter away, especially if the person is in a legally protected category.

The bottom line is to treat employees the way you would want to be treated if the shoe were on the other foot. Give them every opportunity to succeed. Follow up so they always know where they stand. If it comes to termination, do not let it be a surprise. Above all, throughout the process, show respect.

One Last Thing

On very rare occasions, you will deal with an employee who is physically threatening, prone to angry outbursts, or other dangerous behavior. When this happens, never take chances, even if it means bringing in the police.

Summary

People are your organization's greatest asset, your largest expense, and your greatest liability; therefore, helping them work at full capacity is worth whatever time investment it takes on your part.

Making a hiring mistake has a devastating effect on an organization; therefore, it is critical to take the time and follow the proper processes to get hiring right. This is not an exact science, but digging deep to try to understand a candidate is important.

Media organizations that do not represent the communities they serve are poorly positioned for success. We are in a highly competitive business that is judged by our end users. Understanding those users is a baseline for success.

Television stations operate on publicly owned licenses; therefore, government regulation is a reality. Make sure you understand and follow all mandated regulations.

Not being honest with a person who is failing in his job is an unconscionable thing to do. Always tell the truth. If a person who reports to you does not know he is doing a bad job until he receives his annual appraisal, shame on you.

The termination process is complex and time consuming, but cutting corners can result in a lawsuit. Former employees sue because they feel deeply disrespected. Suing is a complex and multiyear process that a former employee must be highly motivated to take. Make sure you do not give them that motivation.

Key Takeaways

- Employees are your most important asset, your greatest expense, and your biggest potential liability.
- Hiring decisions are among the most important you will make. Take the time to do the job right.
- A workforce that reflects the makeup of the community you serve gives you a competitive advantage.
- Employees should always know where they stand, not just during formal reviews.
- Terminated employees must be highly motivated to sue. Showing respect during the termination process removes some of that motivation.

15

CRISIS MANAGEMENT

All broadcasters have war stories, and I'm no exception, but I've tried to keep them out of this book. I'm making an exception in this chapter because it is a real-life example of what happens when disaster strikes a television station. It is from my time managing WXII, the NBC affiliate in the Piedmont Triad.

It was a beautiful Sunday morning in North Carolina. My wife was out of town, and I was cruising down I-40 on my way to church when my cell rang. It was Barry Klaus, our news director. I was surprised, especially since I knew Barry was spending the weekend in New York.

"It's Barry. I just found out Tolly Carr got drunk last night, ran over a pedestrian, and killed him. He refused the Breathalyzer, so they took him to jail and got a court order to take blood. One of our production assistants was in the car but apparently not injured. I'm on my way to LaGuardia to catch a flight home."

I was stunned. "Do you know anything else?"

"I got what I have from the desk. They're checking."

"OK," I said. "I'm going to the station. Meet you there."

For the next few minutes, I just kept driving down the interstate until it occurred to me that I should turn around. I picked the phone up and called David Barrett, the CEO of Hearst Television, but got his voice mail. I then called Phil Stolz, my group head, who was having breakfast with his wife. Phil said he would notify everyone in New York, including our corporate attorneys.

Just before I got to the station, a call came in from a blind number. It was Tolly. He was in tears and could barely speak.

"I'm so sorry," he said.

I asked where he was. He had trouble getting any words out. I said, "Tolly, go home and stay there. You need to find a good attorney to advise you before you talk to me or anyone else."

He said, "OK," and hung up.

Tolly Carr was our weekday morning anchor. In the six months he had been at the job, our viewership had soared with higher ratings among younger women than the other stations combined. Beginning as a photographer right out of college, Tolly had worked his way into sports and, finally, on air. When we held auditions for a morning anchor position, Tolly applied. He was not a traditional anchor, but he did have a quiet manner that made him easy to relate to. The only reason we put Tolly in the focus groups was out of courtesy to a current employee. He won hands down.

Before we gave him the anchor job, Barry and I had a serious conversation about the responsibility of being an anchor. Because he was young and single, we knew there were temptations in his path. We told him to stay away from bars and alcohol, to not be involved with anything that might compromise his reputation, and above all, to remember he represented the television station. Obviously, it had not worked out that way.

Tolly's co-anchor was Kimberly Van Scoy, a veteran professional who had been our evening co-anchor before moving to mornings. Tolly and Kimberly immediately bonded and became good friends. Viewers related to their chemistry, and ratings began to grow.

Tolly and Kimberly became so comfortable with each other that they sometimes joked about their age difference. It was good-spirited but inappropriate, so I sat Tolly down and asked him to stay away from age. The next morning, he said to Kimberly on the air, "They told me to not make fun of your age anymore, so I won't." She loved it.

All these things were on my mind as I pulled into the station. We had found magic in a bottle, but none of that mattered now.

When I got to the office, I called each of the department heads, told them what happened, and asked them to come in. We needed to get all hands on deck.

By early that afternoon, everyone was in, including Barry, who had found a direct flight. We had very little information, and everyone was still in shock; at least I had been able to take some time and think about our next steps. I told everyone we needed to be on the same page, including understanding what was important. "Our morning ratings are probably gone, but we can rebuild morning news. What we can't rebuild is our credibility if we handle this wrong. We are going to be completely transparent and report everything we learn."

I asked Barry which of our senior reporters was least likely to have a relationship with Tolly. He said Bill O'Neil. I told Barry to put Bill and a senior photographer on the story full-time. We had an inherent conflict of interest covering the story, so I told Barry to give Bill independent authority to fully investigate and report without approval from anyone in management. Barry was to also give Bill direct access to our company lawyers rather than going through the usual chain of command.

"If we are going to survive this, it will be because we had total transparency. Bill has to own this story no matter where it takes him."

Reporters from other news organizations were already calling, so I wrote a statement and had the lawyers vet it. It said we were devastated by the tragedy and our hearts went out to the families of everyone involved. I promised WXII 12 would fully report the story and disclose all facts as we learned them. Later that day, O'Neil asked to interview me. I said pretty much the same thing on camera.

One missing piece was Kimberly Van Scoy, who had just left the previous day on vacation. By the time we tracked Kimberly down, she had already heard the news. She said, "I'm coming back and will go on the air tomorrow morning."

I said, "Kimberly, don't do that. We are going to have someone else anchor."

She said, "I can't do that to anyone else. I need to be there."

The next day, we had the most unusual morning news I've ever experienced. We took everyone off the show except Kimberly and meteorologist Austin Caviness. At the beginning of each news block, Kimberly would read the story, followed by a package telling all the gory details. We also showed Tolly's booking picture. When we went to break, she would collapse on the desk in tears. By the end of the break, she would have herself together enough to read the story again. This happened time after time for three days. On Wednesday afternoon, she said to me, "I can't do this anymore." I told her I understood and she did not have to go on again. A few minutes later, she called back to say she felt a responsibility to go on. The next morning, she was back on the air doing it all again.

People at the station were devastated, so I called a meeting to tell them what we knew. I also told them they did not have to cut off their personal relationships with Tolly, but we did not want anyone who had a personal relationship with him involved with the story on any level. We had to make sure we covered the story straight, no matter where that might take us.

A fascinating and completely unexpected thing happened that week. Because this was a huge story, ratings actually went up and stayed up. Viewers felt Kimberly's pain and bonded with her in a way that had never happened before. Kimberly's courage in dealing with what was to her a very personal tragedy earned the respect of our entire staff and caused her to become a newsroom leader. I've never seen anything like it before or since.

Just when we thought the story couldn't get bigger, at his arraignment, Tolly pleaded not guilty. Because the facts were so overwhelming, we had assumed he would probably enter into some kind of plea agreement. The fact he had pleaded not guilty meant the story would now go on for months. Not only did that mean coverage would continue but we also had to make a decision about his employment. Had he pleaded guilty, we would have terminated him, but a not guilty plea changed things.

How we handled his employment situation was important, because it would set precedent for the future. After getting legal advice, I decided to suspend Tolly without pay rather than immediately terminate him. There was no way I would ever let him be on our air again, but because he pleaded not guilty, I felt an obligation to let him have his day in court. This was an internal personnel decision, so not something we could announce. Over the following months, reporters repeatedly asked me if Tolly had been fired. I always told them the same thing. We never discuss personnel issues.

It would be hard to overstate just how big a story this was in our community. It had all the dramatic elements of a soap opera. Young television anchor, dead victim, grieving family, alcohol abuse, a not guilty plea that seemed to go against the facts. The local papers and the other stations could not seem to get enough of the story. A year or so later, after all this was behind us, I went back and counted the number of stories our station had run on air and posted on the web. We had done more than the other stations combined.

Another surprise was the affection viewers still seemed to

hold for Tolly. They saw it as a tragic mistake of judgment. Because of our openness, the station was seen as a victim. Not the outcome one would expect.

Early in the process, I considered hiring a local PR agency to help with communications, but I eventually decided against it. It just didn't feel right to try to position a message. Anything we might say that appeared as if we were defending ourselves would have been a mistake. I believe not doing that was the central reason people saw us as a victim, not a company trying to paint a picture.

Among the bizarre things that happened over the following months was a social media rumor that Tolly had committed suicide. There was no basis for this, but it caught on like wildfire. The switchboard was jammed with calls. When our operator told people the story was not true, they did not believe her. Several said they had heard it on the radio. We were never able to find any evidence of that, but people believed it nonetheless.

As the day went on, people began to come to the station. One woman said, "I know it happened. Why don't you admit it?" Tearful people jammed the emergency room at Wake Forest Baptist Medical Center because the rumor said that was where Tolly's body had been taken. Twice that day, police officers in different communities stopped our news cars to say how sorry they were to hear about Tolly.

We also heard from a large number of people who thought we should give Tolly his job back and an equally large number who thought we shouldn't. We didn't ask for these opinions, but for some reason, people wanted to give them.

As the date of Tolly's trial approached, we made a decision to air the trial live. We were saved from doing that when Tolly suddenly pleaded guilty. He was sentenced to prison.

Because Tolly had few assets, the victim's family was able to collect very little. The station endured investigation by the family's attorneys, but they could find no evidence of liability on our part. I can only imagine what the result would have been if a station car had been involved.

As the years went by, the story faded as those things do. I had not spoken with Tolly since that Sunday morning but did hear reports of him working to put his life back together after he got out of prison. To their credit, some of our employees who had been close to Tolly kept up their relationships. I heard at one point Tolly did some fill-in work at a station in Charlotte, but that did not turn into a job.

One year just before Christmas, I got a call from Tolly. He said, "I never really apologized to you for what I did. I'm calling to finally say I'm sorry."

I said I was sorry too. "You know, Tolly, you still have a lot of friends here. If you are in the neighborhood, feel free to stop by."

There was a pause. "You mean I'm not barred from the building?"

"Of course not. You paid a big price for a big mistake. Come by anytime."

He choked up and said good-bye.

Not only did ratings never drop during the whole saga, they actually went up. Station ratings had been on the upswing anyway, and that was not affected. WXII eventually became the number-one station in the market not just in the morning but in every time period.

Looking back, I believe the single most important thing we did was to make sure the station was open and transparent about everything that happened. Fully reporting the story ourselves went a long way toward saving our relationships with viewers. In fact, it earned their trust. Some negative things did come out, such as the news one of our other employees was in the car and still another had been with Tolly in the bar, but those things did not linger.

I hope you never go through anything like this, but you will have to manage crisis on some level. When that happens, always think of the long-term effect of everything you do. Don't cover anything up. Don't skew the facts. Don't blame others, and above all, don't be defensive. Let the chips fall where they may. After all, you are in the news business.

Summary

You never know when devastating news will come or what it will be about, so there is no way to prepare. What you can do is make sure you are careful to gather the facts and make logical decisions.

As soon as possible, let your boss know what is happening. You don't want him or her to hear the news from anyone else. That would be unfair to your boss as well as hurt your future relationship.

Getting guidance from an appropriate attorney is critical, as is making sure all of your managers are on the same page. Don't be a lone ranger. You have many resources to call on. Use them.

Make sure your staff knows what is going on. Because of legalities, there are some things you may not be able to talk about, but answer as many questions as possible. Your staff wants to know that you are in charge and dealing with the situation. That will give them the comfort level they need to go forward.

Transparency, honest news coverage, and making sure you own the story are important. Some embarrassing things will come out, but better the public gets that from your station than from someone else. Maintaining the trust of your viewers is the single most important thing you can do. Don't skirt any facts or hide any information.

Keep perspective. Whatever is going on will someday be just a memory. Make sure it is a memory in which you can be proud of your actions.

Key Takeaways

- You are running a news organization. The value of the organization is based on the level of trust consumers have in you. Every action you take must maintain that trust.
- Be transparent and tell the truth. Skirting the facts or hiding information will end in disaster.
- Make sure everyone is on the same page with the same understanding of what is going on.
- Keep your boss fully informed. This is his or her crisis too.
- Retain perspective. Remember this is just a part of the big picture.

16

COMMUNITY SERVICE

The fundamental difference between local television stations and the national networks is we are directly connected to our communities. We live with, work with, and have relationships with the people we serve. We cannot ignore their views.

People who live in New York and Los Angeles program networks. Living in those environments naturally affects how programmers see the world in general and programming in particular. They are well aware that their product is going to a national audience made up of people from every part of the nation, and they attempt to produce programs with wide appeal, but make no mistake, the professional and social communities they live in heavily influence their work.

Management and staff of local television stations are also influenced by the communities we live in, but there is one important difference. Our success or failure is directly connected to the people we meet and interact with every day. We cannot ignore the wishes of our local viewers the way networks can. If viewers choose to stop consuming our information products, we are out of business.

Keep in mind, too, that because television stations operate

on government licenses, we are charged to operate in the "public interest, convenience and necessity." Networks are not licensed, another important difference in accountability that affects what we put on our air.

As any general manager can tell you, local communities are also vocal. Television is such a personal medium that viewers feel as if they are talking with people they know, friends who come into their homes every day. We get our fair share of extremists and conspiracy theorists, but most of the people we hear from are sincere and representative of others, so what they think can be an important indication of community reaction.

I once hired a sports anchor who was a complete mismatch with the community. The first day he was on the air, we received over two hundred negative calls. Those calls continued for almost two weeks. I became so concerned that I commissioned a quick research study. The results were not good. Viewers hated the guy. He had been on the air less than four months when I paid off the rest of his two-year contract and let him go.

The interesting thing about this episode is the ratings never went down. It was the volume of negative phone calls that indicated a problem.

Answering Calls

As we discussed in the branding chapter, a brand image is built every time we touch a consumer, not just on one of our platforms but during an interaction of any kind. How we serve our communities in direct interaction is one of those touches.

You can say a lot of bad things about me, but you can't accuse me of not returning irate viewer calls. Just listening to the person sometimes works wonders. Time after time, viewers have said they can't believe I called them back. In many cases, we ended up having a positive conversation.

Unfortunately, the reality of retransmission consent negotiations is that television stations sometimes briefly go off cable or satellite systems. When that happens, there is nothing you can say that will mollify an irate caller. But the fact you took the call or called the person back does make a difference.

The first week I worked at a television station, back in the dark ages, I happened to walk through the lobby when the general manager was on the phone with an irate viewer. I noticed the GM's face was red. I'll never forget him yelling into the phone, "Sir, there are two knobs on your set. One turns it off, and the other changes channels. Feel free to use either one!" I don't recommend this approach.

Community Events

Community service is important not just because it does good but because it builds relationships that have an impact on product loyalty and usage. Because a brand is the result of a consumer's total interaction with an organization, community service is at its core a good business decision.

The form community service takes varies from station to station. It's probably safe to say most stations don't have a specific plan as to how they will serve their viewers. Most are an amalgamation of projects and PSAs. Almost every station has particular events, such as food drives, that they support every year.

However you choose to do community service, make sure you do it right. If being part of an event means you will have an empty booth or tent for a good part of the day, you might be better off passing on that event. Just putting people in the booth is not enough. Be sure your talent is showcased. Just meeting an anchor seen on TV can cause a person to start watching. If the anchor takes the time to smile and say hello, so much the better.

But if the anchor is aloof, distracted, or appears uncomfortable, damage can be done to your brand.

Nonprofit Boards

Most stations have a long history of anchor involvement in local organizations. Advocacy for good works is good for everyone.

There is also a long history of having a station's general manager involved in community organizations. Serving on the boards of organizations such as United Way, Salvation Army, and the chamber of commerce is an excellent way to connect with other high-profile executives, a number of whom will also be clients. Your time is, of course, limited, so be thoughtful about which organizations to join. One tip: boards have meetings; committees do work, so the fewer committees you are on, the better.

Redefining Community Service

All the things we just discussed, from community events to public service announcements, are good things. But just how effective are they at building a brand? If a station is doing a half dozen community events each year and its anchors are doing another half dozen appearances, do consumers really take notice?

Remember that we are dealing with very busy consumers who sometimes feel overwhelmed by the world they live in. They deal with this constant inflow of information by no longer seeing things that are not relevant to their lives. Do they really notice a one-day book drive a station is supporting?

I'm not advocating we drop all these things. That would create a backlash that would hurt the brand. But what if we carefully reduced the number of things we do so that massive resources could be put into one or two high-impact events each year? I call this strategy the big event.

The Big Event

In the chapter on strategic planning, we discussed WXII's Flight of Honor campaign. The station made a public commitment to send every World War II veteran in the viewing area to Washington, DC. It was a big commitment with a big result.

It would have been easy for the station to sponsor and raise the money for one flight. That would have been a good thing to do. Being live at the airport for both the departure and arrival would have also been good. But those things would not have made it a big event.

Flight of Honor was a big event because the station promised to send every veteran to Washington who wanted to go. The station then covered every departure and every return live. This concentrated emphasis is what caught the public's attention and allowed the station and its Rotary partners to raise over $650,000 to fulfill the commitment.

Big events are not easy to create. They require a cause so important it will touch a community's heart. A strong partner to do the organization and legwork is also required. It also needs to be more than just one day. Otherwise, the viewer might not even notice.

No two big events are exactly the same, so there is not a formula to follow. Nor can you necessarily create a big event out of thin air. It begins with some core need in a community. Something people want to be a part of. Above all, it needs to be big.

One-Time Opportunities

Leaders lead, so when major disasters strike or some other emergency need occurs, be prepared to move quickly. One-day telethons are most effective if they are done immediately. So are appeals for food, clothing, water, or whatever other goods are needed.

Let's say a tornado devastates a community. Most stations in your market will eventually do something to help, but it usually takes a few days. Let's say you decide to do a telethon to raise money for people who lost their homes. First, you have to find a partner, such as the Red Cross. Then you have to figure out telephones and other technical details.

If you are going to be the market leader, all those things should be planned before you need them. Talk with the Red Cross and get a commitment to work together on big needs. Figure out the technical details far in advance.

Getting on the air first—and big—is well worth the effort. By the time the other stations do their own thing, they will look like the followers they are.

Always Lead

Whatever you choose to do in community service, always lead. Do not follow another station's lead. Go your own way. Done properly, community service is a competitive advantage.

Summary

Local television stations are directly responsible to the people they serve. Ignoring end users is not an option. Our success or failure is directly connected to their use of our products.

Never dodge viewer calls. Always return the calls of viewers who leave messages. You may not be able to mollify the viewer, but you can demonstrate respect and make clear that you care about the viewer's opinions.

Doing a lot of little things can get lost in the noise. Focusing on one or two big events will have much greater impact, both in solving a community need and in advancing a station's brand value.

Leaders always lead. By preplanning response to emergencies, including appropriate partnerships, a station can vault ahead of competitors who drag their feet.

Never follow a competitor's lead. Always go your own way.

Key Takeaways

- Respect the opinions of viewers. They likely represent many others.
- Always take advantage of the opportunity to speak with viewers, especially when they have a complaint.
- Big events have big impact. Smaller events get lost in the noise of daily life.
- Always lead. Go your own way.

17

Boomers and Turnarounds

There are many kinds of television stations, but two in particular offer opportunities for great leaders to shine: boomers and turnarounds. Boomers are stations currently in first place but vulnerable. Turnarounds are last-place stations that would like to be first.

The most important thing that determines the future of both boomers and turnarounds is leadership. No matter how strong a station, no matter how committed the owner, nothing has more effect on the daily success or failure of a station than the leader. Of course, if the owner decides to milk the station dry, any boomer will get in trouble. But I know of at least one boomer that has survived more than one bad owner because the leader is both outstanding and committed to the long-term success of the station.

In the case of a turnaround, leadership is equally critical. Turnarounds are so difficult and the success rate is so small that very few ever go the distance. Of course, an owner willing to invest proper time and resources is also critical, but an owner cannot turn a station around. That takes a leader.

Great leaders are rare. The history of television is littered with managers who thought hiring the right talent away from a competitor or creating a great marketing plan would either fix a station in trouble or take one from last place to first. There are no magic bullets, no easy fixes, and no simple solutions. This is a business in which pressure to succeed is intense. Managers are constantly under the spotlight, both by corporate and their own staffs. The temptation to find a shortcut always awaits, but shortcuts usually just make things worse.

Part of the frustration in leading a decaying boomer or a last-place station is that nothing happens fast. Boomers take years to decay. Turnarounds take years to succeed. The landscape is constantly shifting but at a glacial pace. Viewer habits and loyalties take so long to change that leaders sometimes feel like they are treading water.

Human optimism also plays a part. Slowly decaying ratings are easy to dismiss by a leader who does not understand why viewership is declining. Turnarounds take years of slow growth, interspersed with occasional backward moves that can so discourage a general manager the staff also becomes discouraged.

Although the challenges of boomers and turnarounds are completely different, the single most important leadership quality required for success in either is exactly the same: the ability to articulate a vision that people believe in and want to achieve.

Leading a Boomer

Boomers are successful stations that have dominated their market's news ratings over many decades. Because network program ratings reflect local news ratings, boomers also have strong network performance. In all cases, boomers have deep roots in their communities forged over all those years.

Every company would love to own boomers because of their ability to produce profits. They are also prestigious positions for their general managers, but keeping a boomer on top can be one of the most difficult jobs in the business.

It is very easy for management and staff alike to assume that because their station has been number one "forever," that is their rightful place. This leads to complacency and product stagnation. "Our news has always been number one and always will be. Don't mess with success," is a common theme.

Because there is an inverse ratio between profitability and appetite for risk, the temptation is to invest little, if any, effort or money advancing the product. Far easier to simply continue to fund what has worked in the past, adding whatever current fad is in vogue along the way.

There is also little incentive for boomers to create a forward-looking strategic plan. By their nature, plans involve change, and no one likes change, especially when things are going well.

The nice thing about boomers is they really don't have to change as long as market competitors accept their secondary positions. Surprisingly, there are still a few markets where this is the case.

If you are running a boomer in a market where everyone else accepts the status quo, then good for you. Spend your time controlling expenses and being involved in the community. But what happens when one of your competitors is bought by a company unwilling to accept the status quo?

I've been on both sides of this equation and have observed great commonality in the response of boomers to pressure from another station. They go in stages something like this:

Unconcern—"We are the market standard. Bring it on."

Belittlement—"They call that news? Good luck."

Denial—"This change in ratings is an aberration. It can't be right."

Deeper Denial—"Those guys must be cheating. Maybe they are doing something with the Nielsen rules."

Panic—"We've got to do something!" This is usually followed by a knee-jerk reaction.

Magic Bullets—"Let's buy a . . ." Magic bullets never work.

Copying—"Let's add the things that are working for those guys." Boomers that copy a formerly belittled station guarantee morale in their own newsroom is destroyed.

Loss of Identity—Change for the sake of change and copying a competitor both muddle a station's brand, almost always starting a downhill spiral that ends badly.

Failure—Once a boomer fails, it almost never rises from the dead.

None of this has to happen.

The path to making sure a boomer continues to be a boomer is to begin with an honest analysis. How much of your viewership is based on habit? How much is based on the fact your competitors do a bad job? Most importantly, what are your real strengths and how do you reinforce them?

A boomer that is executing a strong strategic plan that evolves its product in a logical way is able to prepare for the future. Because the plan is long term, changes can be made incrementally without jarring viewers. A boomer that is not taking its position for granted can be a hard thing to beat. There are a number of these around the country. WEEK in Peoria is an interesting example because the station has survived numerous owners, yet continued to dominate. A closer look shows that general manager Mark DeSantis has been there the entire time. Leadership has made the difference.

Boomer Culture

Part of the reason a boomer is a boomer is an internal culture of belief in the station and its mission in the community. The worst thing you can do to that culture is to parachute in some consultants with the latest, greatest product idea for throwing the old out the window and putting in something completely new.

The first problem is that the staff does not think anything is wrong, so they naturally resist change. That often leads to half in, half out, layering the new over the old. I'd love to have a buck for every time I've heard someone at a declining boomer say, "Everything was just fine until they started to make changes."

The core problem is that you cannot change product without first adjusting culture.

The key to culture is to begin with understanding and acknowledging its strengths. Maybe those dull on-set interviews actually do have a place somewhere in the product. The leader then has to lay out two visions for the future. The first is what will happen if the product does not evolve. The second vision is how the station can create the future using the current culture as a foundation, not something to throw out. Boomers have a culture that says they are already the leaders; therefore, they respond to messages that advance that leadership. Fearmongering does not work. The response to fear is always to throw up cultural walls.

Unfortunately, when thinking about transitioning a boomer, most leaders leave the rank-and-file staff out of the equation, assuming management can simply make changes at will. Nothing works without staff buy-in. The best way to gain that buy-in is to explain what is happening and why, then lay out a vision for the future that is both exciting and a logical progression of the current product.

Show me a station that has staff buy-in of a strong strategic plan, not dependent on what any other station is doing, and I'll show you either a boomer or a station that will eventually become a boomer. The most successful stations go their own way, executing their own game plan, without regard to what anyone else does. They respect competitors but do not react to them. Above all, they always advance their product.

Leading a Turnaround

Before you take on the immense job of leading a turnaround, make sure two things are in place. First, the station must have hit bottom. Anything less than bottom leaves cultural walls in place that waste energy and destroy focus.

Second, you must have an owner willing to invest in the future. You can't buy your way to success in this business, but you must have proper funding. Turnarounds take years to complete, so you must have an owner who is also patient.

There is no single way to lead a turnaround, but here is the process I've developed over the years that has had success in a number of places:

Begin with Operational Excellence

Michael Porter, a strategist at Harvard, calls operational excellence "the price of admission." Operational excellence means creating a great newscast that does everything right—from talent to set to graphics, the newscast hits on all cylinders. In the past, when stations just competed against other stations, doing a better job was sometimes enough to win. Those days are long gone. You can't beat a boomer by simply doing a better job.

Belief

If you are doing a great job, sooner or later, you will begin to have some kind of wins. They may not be ratings wins but things your staff believes they are doing better than anyone else. Once you have belief, build on that belief by expanding the thing you do well.

Strategy

It sounds strange to suggest saving strategy until after operational excellence and belief, but it's actually very logical. Forming a strategy with no underpinnings is not much more than a hope and a prayer. Strategy must be based on some kernel of belief.

Big Ideas

With strategy in place, you need occasional things to create a stir among viewers, getting the attention of those who do not normally watch you. A big idea is something that either makes viewer's lives better or significantly enhances the community. Big ideas are not about the station; they are about the viewer and the community. For instance, helping build a children's hospital in a community that does not have one is a big idea.

Where do big ideas come from? They are already in your community and waiting to be brought to life. Just look around.

The single most important thing to do when leading a turnaround is to ignore your competitors. Constantly execute your plan without regard to what anyone else does. My position has always been that our station is setting a new market standard, not measuring ourselves by what others do.

I've also found it best to not try to measure success by ratings. In the end, ratings will come, but first, you have to be able to know that you are building a brand you and your staff believe in.

Never make things seem better or easier than they are. Ratings go up, and ratings go down. They never move in a straight line. Don't run through the building jumping for joy when ratings go up, because at some point, they will also dip. You need to be as upbeat and positive during the dips as you are during growth.

Mind-Set

As we discussed in an earlier chapter, the place to start with any leadership challenge is your own mind-set. Leading any station into the future is a multiyear process with both highs and lows. Staff attitudes will key off your attitude, so never allow yourself to create unrealistic expectations. You need to be constantly positive but also levelheaded.

Not everything you try will succeed. There will be failures along the way. When that happens, acknowledge the failure, be able to articulate what you have learned as a group, then move on.

Consistent Leadership

Whether you are running a boomer or doing a turnaround, remember that success begins and ends with your leadership. No one else can take on this responsibility. Success is ultimately what you get paid for.

Summary

Boomers are longtime number-one stations that dominate their market's ratings. Turnarounds are last-place stations that want to be in first place. While their challenges are on the opposite ends of the spectrum, they share a common need for effective leadership.

The culture of a boomer makes it very difficult to change the station's direction. Making major changes to a boomer without staff buy-in can lead to disaster. Far better to build a strategy based on current station strengths that the staff will accept and embrace.

Turning a last-place station around is one of the most difficult management challenges a leader will ever face. Most turnarounds fail. Those that succeed require great leadership, an effective plan, and an owner willing to commit both reasonable resources and reasonable time.

If a boomer is not challenged by other stations in the market, it has no incentive to modernize and advance its product.

Not every initiative you try will succeed. When that happens, acknowledge the failure, learn what you can, and then move on.

Whatever your challenge as a leader, create a strategy and a game plan that goes your own way. Do not copy other stations or use them as a standard of success. Doing so concedes leadership of your station to someone else.

Key Takeaways

- Boomers are longtime first-place stations.
- Turnarounds are last-place stations that want to be in first place.
- Regardless of a station's position, its culture is its strongest force.
- Always go your own way. Never make a competitor your standard.
- Leadership is always the most important key to success.

18

RISK-TAKING

The primary reason television news has become so homogenized is that no one wants to risk hurting a formula that has worked. That was fine back in the days before fragmentation and direct consumer communication changed the playing field, but today's field is in constant flux.

As we continue to see constant development of elements that use consumer time, it is clear that eventually some stations will have to exit local news simply because the audience will not justify the cost of producing product. If it were not for today's multistream revenue models, the thinning out would have already been much further along.

Alternate ways of serving our customers—ways that go beyond simply putting television product on mobile, web, OTT, and other platforms—must be developed, both for leading stations that want to grow and those in trouble that want to survive.

During the heyday of television news, any station, no matter how poor the ratings, could make money in news. That model can still work today, provided the same owner programs multiple market stations with the same product, but a stand-alone station with poor revenue and high news-production costs stopped making sense some time ago.

If the station you lead is in so precarious a position that you are willing to embark on a major risk, you need to know that big risks are rarely successful. That does not mean you should give up and not try. Your risk may pay off. But before you gamble, make sure you have tried everything else. I've been in that position, so it might be helpful to share my experience.

A Case Study

When I took over WBBM, the CBS-owned station in Chicago, news ratings were in last place. Even worse, the profit margin was around 14 percent, an embarrassment for a network station in the nation's third-largest market. My third month in the job, the station actually lost $180,000.

I was well aware of how bad things were at WBBM before taking the job, but coming off success at KARE 11 in Minneapolis, I was looking for a big challenge and found it.

The next four years were spent cleaning up the operation and building a modern newscast. Bringing expenses in line and recharging the sales department eventually raised the profit margin to an acceptable level, but ratings did not move.

Part of the problem was WBBM's history as a former leading station that had made a series of disastrous mistakes over multiple decades. Some of the more notable debacles included the Operation PUSH boycott of the 1980s, Bill Kurtis's disastrous return from New York after failing there, and Bill Applegate's more recent foray into bleeding tabloid news. These high-profile fiascos had poisoned the water, especially among WBBM's formerly loyal African American audience, who had moved to WLS. WBBM's equally loyal upscale north-side viewers had chosen WMAQ.

We had tried all the normal things one does to make a station successful. We could probably have written a book on conventional ways to try to improve a television newscast. I suppose we could have simply tried to hang on, but neither news director Pat Costello nor I were wired that way. We would rather fail big than simply peter out.

I had kept my job for the previous four years by improving the station's profit margin from 14 percent to 42 percent, but news ratings never got out of the tank. Pat and I liked our anchor team of Lester Holt and Linda MacLennan, but they had never been able to break through and attract viewers. We had tried all the standard things and many others that were not standard. A different kind of newscast with Carol Marin, who I still have immense respect for, was our last shot.

Carol was a revered anchor who had quit her job at WMAQ rather than co-anchor with Jerry Springer. I had hired Carol to be an investigative reporter and shared her services with *60 Minutes.* Carol did not want to go back to the anchor desk, but our promise of a no-frills, straight-to-the-point newscast finally convinced her.

The program struck a spark with journalists and got national attention. CBS and PBS did profiles. Walter Cronkite and Dan Rather both publicly endorsed the newscast, as did TV critics around the country. *Broadcasting & Cable* magazine even named me a Fifth Estater for local news innovation. There was only one problem. The program failed.

The one saving grace of the *Ten O'Clock News with Carol Marin* was it provided important lessons that led to the success of my next two turnarounds, both of which involved innovation.

If you are going to fail, at least learn something from it. Here are several things I learned that have helped make subsequent efforts more successful.

Innovate from Strength

Risk-taking at weak television stations almost never works, usually because some form of innovation is used as a last hope, a magic bullet after everything else has failed. Innovation is the long shot. It is a big idea one hopes will change everything else. Neither life nor television works that way.

Effective innovation must come from strength. That means doing the hard work of creating a sound organization and superb product before stepping into unchartered territory, something Michael Porter at Harvard calls operational excellence.

If you have not first built a solid foundation, innovation becomes just a distraction, a way to feel you are doing your best. Doing your best does not employ people and pay the light bill.

Innovation Must Be Difficult

Any effort that is not difficult is probably not truly innovative. In fact, it is not risk-taking at all. If something is easy to achieve, your competitors will immediately copy it, taking away any advantage you may have gained. Whatever you are trying to achieve, it must be so difficult that competitors will be unwilling, or culturally unable, to match it.

Many years ago, a station in Saint Louis started a campaign called 24 Hour News. Hard to believe that news hasn't always been twenty-four hours a day, but in its time, 24 Hour News was an innovation. The station's competitors and other stations immediately copied the campaign across the nation. Because every station was doing it, the idea became meaningless.

An even better example is the breaking news crawls television stations started running at the bottom of their newscasts after 9/11. Soon, every station in America was running crawls across the bottom of their newscasts. Some still do so today. Was it a good idea? Who knows? But it was easy to copy, so any value viewers perceived it to have was quickly dissipated among stations.

Long-Term Commitment Is Essential

Nothing hard is quick. The most successful forms of innovation come about over a long period of time and eventually become part of a station's DNA. This is important because, like the level of difficulty involved, no competitor will be willing to invest that same amount of time to match the effort.

Innovation that is hard to do and developed over several years can be impossible for any other station to match.

True Innovation Involves Financial Risk

The inverse relationship between profit and risk means stations on top are rarely interested in innovation, yet these are the very stations who should be leading with fresh thinking and new ideas. Only successful stations possess the audience launchpad and financial resources that true innovation requires. If innovation can be done without financial risk, there is likely little financial reward.

Why should dominant stations care about innovation? Because linear newscast audiences continue to age. The time has come to stop accepting the status quo.

Clearly Defined Business Goals

If you are going to put the time, effort, and money into a project to make sure it is successful, be certain that you are also making the best use of station resources. Is this idea really worth the risk? Are we sure the payoff is sufficient? Just having a great idea that everyone believes will advance the product is not enough. What is the business case?

Remember, only the consumer has the ability to decide if something will succeed or fail. Business goals must be about the consumer.

Know the Limits

If you are going to invest years of time and substantial resources, make sure you have intermediate goals along the way. If something is not working, know when to shut it down.

Don't Scare Viewers

Disrupting viewers is a bad place to start. Doing something that shocks viewers, such as suddenly removing sports from the 6:00 p.m. news, can create barriers that are rarely overcome. Remember that viewers have been watching conventional newscasts for decades. Even their kids and grandkids, who may not be loyal television news viewers, still believe they know what a television newscast looks like. Their expectations are conditioned.

If you are going to make radical change, be sure that it does not look like radical change at the outset. This sounds like a dichotomy, but it is not. Your goal is to achieve results. Radical change should start slowly and become more innovative along the way. If you do everything at once, you risk alienating consumers.

Avoid "Anticipointment"

A marketing campaign that makes empty promises is worse than no campaign at all.

How often have you seen a television station tout a radical, earthshaking new idea, then tuned in to find out it was just a new news set? How about the big promotion campaign for a new anchor who turns out to be just . . . well, just an anchor?

Only when you are sure something new is providing real viewer-perceived value does a marketing campaign make sense. Otherwise, use marketing to promote the real viewer benefits your newscast offers.

Be Smart

If you are going to do something big, find a way to pretest it. Don't fall in love with an idea to the point you go forward against logic that says not to. It's tough to hear someone call your baby ugly, but if your baby is ugly, better to know at the beginning.

Time after time, I've seen strong, confident leaders make major mistakes because no one on their staffs had the courage to say, "This is a bad idea." If you have set the proper tone in your station, someone will always be willing to diplomatically tell you the truth.

Summary

Successful television stations rarely do true innovation because the risk to current profits seems unreasonable. Investing in a new initiative that does not immediately return a profit is hard to justify when a television station is on top with all cylinders firing.

Risk-taking usually comes only when a station in trouble has tried everything else. Without the user base to support the enterprise, innovation becomes a long shot, a high-risk proposition that is likely to fail.

The best time to take risks is when a station is on top. Not only do the odds of success increase dramatically, but the station has the kind of resources required to do the job right as well as the willingness to stay the course over the long term.

An innovation that is easily copied gives a station no competitive advantage. Anything easy to do, low cost, requiring few resources, and with a quick payoff is neither innovative nor risky. Things such as this more appropriately come under the heading of operational excellence.

Never bet the farm on a high-risk idea. Know when to get out by putting hard metrics in the plan that must be achieved by specific dates.

Viewers have been conditioned over many decades as to what television news looks like. Anything that jars the viewer by radically changing that formula creates unacceptable risk. Radical change must not start out looking like radical change.

Don't fall in love with your pet idea. This is a business. Everything we do must make sense.

Key Takeaways

- Innovate from strength. Risk-taking by weak stations usually fails.
- Be difficult to copy. If it is easy, it is not worth doing.
- Think for the long term. Nothing good happens overnight.
- Have a timetable and clearly defined business goals, and stick to them.
- Know when to get out.
- Do not scare viewers.
- Avoid anticipointment.
- Be smart. Don't fall in love with your ideas.

19

Unions

Nothing in this chapter is designed to give legal advice or take the place of legal counsel. Organized labor is a complex subject with ever-changing rules, so don't take this chapter for more than it is intended, which is simply to give you a sense of the issues a general manager deals with in a union shop.

Why Have Unions?

Why do television stations have unions? Because at some point in the past, employees lost so much trust in management that they were willing to go through the difficult process of forming a union. Make no mistake: unions are a result of management failure.

It's amazing how much misunderstanding there is in our industry about the role of unions in television stations. We've all heard the story of the news director who was not allowed to insert a tape in his office machine (back when we still used tapes), the supervisor who supposedly lost his job because he violated union rules, the threat of dreaded grievance filings.

While there is some truth in all these stories, they are often taken out of context, giving inexperienced managers the impression unions are some mythical force that should not be messed with. Let's begin with some facts.

- A union's power is limited to whatever concessions management agreed to in the most recent contract. If the contract contains illogical rules, that is because management did not do their job at the bargaining table.
- All rules are subject to change during the next negotiation.
- No matter what the contract says, actual practice creates past precedents that can sometimes overrule the contract. In other words, if the employer or the union chooses to not exercise contractual rights, those rights can go away.
- Unions do sometimes protect subpar employees, but again, that is a result of management failure.
- Union employees are no different from other employees. They are human beings who respond positively to effective management.
- The agreed-upon rules apply to both sides. Smart managers who understand a contract can use the rules to their advantage.
- Unions are not necessarily permanent fixtures. Although difficult, it is possible to decertify a union, something I've done twice.

The starting point in dealing with any union is to read and understand the contract. Every contract is the result of a painstaking negotiation, so it is important to understand both the wording and the context. Why is a certain rule in place? Does that rule impede operations, or is it functionally meaningless? Where are the potholes? Opportunities?

When I was running the CBS station in Chicago, we had six different unions in the building. Walking around the first week, I met people who had never met a general manager before. Hard to believe but true. Management had been pretty much hands off, perpetuating an us-versus-them attitude. Management was seen as "the suits."

The result of no relationship between management and employees was out-of-control union rules. For instance, one day, an editing supervisor refused a request to fill in for a sick editor. Instead, he went home. When the new chief engineer I had hired called and asked the supervisor to explain himself, the supervisor said, "I don't edit." The chief had read the contract and knew the supervisor could be required to edit. When he still refused to come back to work, we terminated the employee. The union, of course, filed a grievance, and we went to arbitration.

After hearing both sides, the judge asked to meet with me and the company attorney. He told us that because the station had never before required employees to actually show up for work, past practice required him to reinstate the employee. We had run afoul of the "past practice" rule that says no matter what might be in a contract, if the actual practice is different, the practice takes precedent over the contract.

The supervisor got his job back and back pay for the time he had been out. Our response was to post a notice saying that going forward, all employees were required to show up for work. Several months later, the supervisor pulled the same stunt. We had formally changed our practice, meaning we could now enforce the contract.

Shortly after taking over another station, I read the International Brotherhood of Electrical Workers (IBEW) contract and learned the union only had two weeks to file a grievance, so changing practices might be worth trying. I had our chief engineer begin by training a nonunion employee in master control. No one seemed to notice, so we trained a nonunion person to operate a live truck. No complaints. We then started having production assistants shoot low-priority video. One of the photographers complained but not formally.

A year later, two IBEW representatives asked to meet. They were angry about the changes. I feigned surprise. "I thought you didn't care, which is why we kept expanding. Of course, it's too late. This is how we now do business." They didn't like it, but there was nothing they could do. During the next contract negotiation, we were able to remove all jurisdictional control from the union.

Changing jurisdiction language in the contract was the first chink in the union's armor. Several years later, the membership decertified.

Had the removal of jurisdictional control created an uproar in the station, I would have stopped immediately. Creating a morale problem would be counterproductive to achieving our goal of greater efficiency. The fact no one seemed to notice indicated jurisdictional control was not a big deal to the membership.

Most union members have little idea of the fine details in their contracts. There are always a few who know the rules by heart, but for the most part, even shop stewards are ill-informed.

Organizing Efforts

Union organizers are always on the lookout for new opportunities, but they never target an organization at random. In almost all cases, organizers only invest time in places where employees are unhappy. If your station is experiencing an organizing effort, then shame on you. Something is wrong in the management of your organization.

Employees have every right to form a union, and many of the cards are stacked against the company, so once a vote is scheduled, it may be too late. If you do find yourself facing a vote and win by making promises to change, make sure you actually keep those promises.

The single strongest anti-union tools at your disposal is walking around the building, knowing employees' names, and chatting with employees. If you actually talk with the rank and file, they will tell you everything that is going on in the building. If you find a problem, fix it.

Know the Law

There is more to dealing with the union than just what is in the contract. For instance, you have to be careful to not start a conversation with a union member about the union. If the member brings something up, then fine. But don't put yourself at risk of being accused of tampering. Neither should you take this prohibition too far. You have rights too.

Understanding the law also allows you to maintain the moral high ground, something essential in any negotiation. Your best source for understanding the law is your company attorney or outside counsel.

Right to Work versus Closed Shop

Federal rules concerning unions are the same in all states, but not all states have the same laws. The difference between right to work and closed shop is in who is required to join. In a closed shop state, such as New York, every employee covered by a union contract is required to be a dues-paying member of the union. It is not unusual for a union in a closed shop state to send a note to a station asking that a particular employee be terminated for nonpayment of dues. One goal of all union contract negotiations is to have the station automatically withhold dues payments from employee paychecks. It's easy to see why.

In right-to-work states, employees in union shops can choose to not join the union and not pay dues, putting the union at a significant disadvantage. All the other negotiated rules apply, so employees that do not pay dues are still in the unit and covered by the contract, but without compulsory membership, making the unit viable can be difficult from the union's point of view.

Decertification

Having run two stations in which employees chose to decertify their unions, I can tell you that decertification was never my first goal. My first goal was to create a work relationship between the unionized employees and the company that benefited everyone.

In some cases, a union shop works just fine, but there are also cases where unionized employees feel they would be better off in a normal employee-employer relationship. If enough members of a bargaining unit feel they would be better off without representation, then it is possible for them to go through a legal process to decertify the unit.

The most important thing for you to know about decertification is that the process begins and ends with the employees in the unit, not with the company. Decertification is a difficult, time-consuming, and disruptive process that can lead to hard feelings between employees.

Remember that unions are the result of employees not trusting management, so building trust is an important part of your job, as it is with every other employee, union or not. If a unit chooses to decertify, it means they trust management. Trust is your goal.

Like every other part of your relationship with station unions, make sure your labor attorney keeps you up-to-date on the law. If in doubt, always speak with your attorney before doing anything.

Priorities

Your top priorities in a union shop are no different from your priorities in a nonunion shop. You want everyone on the same page and working to achieve the same goals. If a union is interfering with your ability to do that, then negotiating a better contract becomes critically important.

Most importantly, remember this. A contract is a reflection of the level of trust employees have in you and the company you work for. Unions are a result of poor management or working conditions, not an inherent desire to bargain collectively. You have much more control in this area than you may think.

Above all, know your rights and know employee rights. That means getting advice exclusively from your labor attorney. It also means knowing your contract as well as knowing the law. Do not allow yourself to become intimidated as so many managers have done. Knowledge is strength.

Summary

There is broad misunderstanding in our industry about the role unions actually play in a television station. For this reason, some general managers are intimidated by unions, fearful of making some kind of legal mistake. There is no reason for this to happen.

A union contract is a negotiated agreement between management and a bargaining unit that defines the working relationship between the two. Unions only have whatever power a company has agreed to during the bargaining process. Reading and understanding the contract is a critical part of your job.

If you are unhappy with the rules in a particular contract, you have the opportunity to correct that unhappiness during the next contract negotiation. This does not mean you will necessarily get everything you want. Both sides are required to negotiate fairly, seeking common ground.

Union employees are no different from any other employees and should be treated as such. Like with other employees, you want to build trust.

In some cases, union members choose to dissolve their unit in a decertifying process. This process is initiated and controlled by members of the unit, not the company.

The most important thing you can do in regard to unions is to understand the contract and the law. That means leaning on your labor attorney for counsel and advice. Don't believe what you hear from other people. Trust and listen to your attorney.

Key Takeaways

- Unions are the result of past management failure.
- Union employees should be treated like all other employees.
- When dealing with unions, make sure you know the law and the contract.
- If you are unhappy with a contract, you have the opportunity to change it during the next negotiation.
- Trust and listen to your labor attorney.

20

NETWORK RELATIONS

When I first became a general manager, stations individually negotiated network agreements, including compensation. Today, those agreements are always done on a group level, including what was originally called reverse compensations but is now usually referred to as network programming payments. How all this came about is worth understanding.

The relationship between independently owned stations and their networks has a stormy history that, ironically, in a time of unlimited video competition, has never been stronger. Some might say "never more codependent."

During the grand era of network radio in the 1930s, networks needed nationwide distribution to make their business models work. To achieve that, they shared a portion of network advertising revenue with affiliated stations. This was called compensation, meaning it compensated stations for the opportunity to sell commercials during network programming. During those days, advertising agencies produced and paid for network programming. Without programming costs, both NBC and CBS became very profitable, so sharing a portion of those profits to ensure stations stayed on the air seemed reasonable.

When television arrived during the late 1940s, the compensations model was transferred to the new medium. The enormous start-up costs for television in the early 1950s meant midsize and smaller stations needed compensation just to survive.

As more and more families began to buy television sets, advertising increased until, by the 1960s, advertising was a larger source of income for most stations than compensation. Still, network compensation remained a critical source of station revenue.

Prior to the 1976 Olympics, ABC was considered a marginal network not in the same class as NBC and CBS. With far fewer affiliates than the other networks, ABC barely competed in the news arena.

The enormous success of the 1976 Olympics, spearheaded by the genius of Roone Arledge, changed everything. For the first time, ABC won prime time. In an equally brilliant move, ABC followed with the record-setting miniseries *Roots*.

Suddenly seeing itself as a major player, ABC tapped Arledge to create a competitive news department that could take on NBC and CBS head-to-head.

With new investments in prime-time programming and a real news department, ABC went affiliate shopping, picking off both NBC and CBS affiliates around the country. Most new affiliates said publicly they were switching to ABC because it was the network of the future. The real reason was more pragmatic. ABC was willing to pay significantly higher compensation rates to sign up key stations.

NBC and CBS, of course, responded. By 1980, compensation rates at all three networks were significantly higher than in the past.

The 1980s and 1990s were high-flying years for both networks and stations. They were also a time when all three networks changed ownership more than once. NBC went from RCA to GE and is today owned by Comcast. CBS went from a stand-alone company to Larry Tisch, then to Westinghouse. ABC was sold to Capital Cities, then eventually to Disney.

The new network owners were not traditionalists afraid to change past practices. With the advertising agency model long gone, the enormous cost of network programming meant networks were not highly profitable enterprises. In fact, network-owned and -operated stations made more profits than their parent networks. Given this climate, owners naturally began to ask why they were still paying compensations to stations.

As network affiliation agreements were renegotiated during those years, rates began to decline. By this time, it was clear that no one network was going to dominate the ratings landscape, so stations became much more circumspect. Affiliation changes became far less common.

As the national economy boomed during the early 1990s, networks continued to lower compensation, with some predicting an end to the practice.

Almost unnoticed during this time was the launch of Rupert Murdoch's Fox network in the late 1980s. Murdoch founded the network on a group of large market-independent stations he bought from John Kluge's Metromedia Company.

Murdoch was so determined to make Fox an actual network that in the fall of 1993, he outbid CBS for the rights to the National Football Conference of the NFL. Murdoch paid what seemed to be an outrageous price because he assumed many CBS affiliates would switch to Fox in order to keep the highly lucrative games on their stations. That did not happen.

With the huge costs of NFL football and prime-time programming, Murdoch began a two-front plan of buying stations and buying affiliations. This caused NBC and CBS to raise their own affiliate compensation rates to protect themselves from Fox.

It was not until the 2000s that compensation levels again dropped. By the recession of 2008/2009, most network contracts were phasing out compensation completely. Fox had gone even further, charging some stations a fee to affiliate.

As we discussed in a previous chapter, the local television business as we know it was saved by the addition of subscriber compensation fees paid by cable and satellite companies. When these fees became real money, networks started to make a not unreasonable case that without a major network, a station would not be in a position to demand subscriber fees. In fact, smaller independent stations as well as nonprofits, such as PBS stations, routinely asserted their rights to "must carry," which ensured carriage but voided their right to demand subscriber fees.

Over time, the percentage of subscriber fees paid by stations to their networks grew to the point a large portion of a station's fees went to their network. There was resentment from the stations, but they had to admit the networks' arrangement made sense. By sharing with the networks, stations ensured network programming and sporting events would stay viable, giving viewers unique reasons to watch local affiliates. The portion of retransmission fees kept by stations still represented a significant revenue source that in some cases challenged advertising for the crown of most profitable stream.

Network Preemptions

Prior to our current era, television stations routinely preempted network programming to run local programs stations found more profitable. CBS, for example, was hard-hit every year by Billy Graham specials. During times of heavy inventory demand, stations would arbitrarily air a local two-hour movie on a weeknight, usually Thursday because of that day's value to retail. This practice was known as make-good theater.

During the mid-1990s, NBC, in the midst of a bidding war with Fox for some of its affiliates, introduced what it called a preemption basket. The basket was a limited number of hours a station could preempt under the terms of the affiliation contract. Later, the basket was split into a regular basket and a sports basket. Eventually, networks and stations agreed that in addition to their basket, stations could also preempt for breaking news events without penalty of the basket.

In today's era of exploding technology, the preemption game has changed. Not only do the networks threaten stations with financial penalties, it is not in the best interest of a station to cover up high-viewership prime-time programming with something that does not advance the station's brand; therefore, preemption of prime time for the sole purpose of providing more sales inventory is rare.

When a station does preempt network programming for something other than breaking news or emergency weather, it is usually for local programming that advances a station's brand.

Affiliation Changes

On occasion, stations sometime change network affiliations, but that is rare. Past turmoil taught stations and networks that stability is best for all. However, this is not a hard rule, especially when networks have the opportunity to buy local stations, something we saw happen in San Francisco, Miami, and Boston, just to name a few.

The General Manager's Role in Network Relations

When I first became a general manager, it was not unusual for stations to preempt network programming that did not, in the manager's opinion, meet community standards. I did this myself on several occasions. In one case, CBS had a program's producer call me to discuss my objections. I don't know that my opinion actually made a difference, but the network was at least responsive.

Today, local stations have almost no control over the content of network programming. That does not mean you, as the leader of a local television station, should not register an objection to something you believe is inappropriate. It is also perfectly proper for you to share viewer reactions to a program with affiliate relations. In fact, you have a responsibility to do so. Networks are East and West Coast businesses. They make decisions based on ratings. Whether the network responds or not, you have a responsibility to act as a voice for your viewers.

Finally, remember that your station and your company are partners with your network. General managers that maintain positive relations with their networks are much better off than those who see the relationship as adversarial. Both you and your network have strong reasons to see to it that each is successful.

Summary

The relationship between networks and stations has continued to evolve throughout the history of broadcasting, usually because one party or the other has the upper hand. The fact is stations and networks need each other. It is in their mutual best interest to cooperate.

Though local general managers have very little input on national programming, general managers still have a responsibility to represent their community standards when giving feedback.

Network compensation was originally a way to share network profits with local stations. As local audiences grew, advertising gradually became much more important, causing networks to seek ways to reduce compensation.

The growth of ABC in the 1970s and the growth of Fox in the 1990s both moved power from networks to stations, resulting in numerous cases of stations changing network affiliations. Time has shown that changing networks rarely brings long-term advantage to a station, so the practice is rare these days. However, networks sometime drop affiliates in favor of network-owned stations.

The advent of retransmission consent has bolstered the financial viability of both stations and their networks.

Network preemptions are much rarer today than in years past, primarily because it is in the best interest of both parties to keep network programming strong.

Though the history of relations between stations and networks has been bumpy, the two organizations need each other. It is in the best interest of a general manager to create a positive working relationship.

Key Takeaways

- The relationship between networks and stations has ebbed and flowed depending on which party has power.
- Though stations would prefer to keep all retransmission compensation, sharing with a network ensures the viability of high-quality programming and major sporting events.
- Preemptions are far less a factor today than in the past for two reasons: network contracts and the vested interest stations have in making network programming successful.
- General managers have a responsibility to represent their community's standards when giving feedback to their network.
- Over the years, networks and stations have often been at odds, but the reality is both parties need each other.

21

REGULATION

The original Communications Act of 1934 and the revised act of 1996 both affirm the unique nature of broadcasting in the United States.

When radio and television were first developed, most countries saw them as national services to be run by government-affiliated organizations. The BBC is a good example. It was only later that privately held stations were allowed.

The United States took a radically different course: the government chose not to be involved in broadcasting. Both radio and television frequencies would be licensed to private individuals and companies, with no government involvement whatsoever in the content of programming. This followed the spirit of the First Amendment to the Constitution in which the independence of free expression and press were imbedded into the very nature of the country.

Under the US system, the government—that is, the citizens—retained ownership of the airways, licensing their use to private parties. In return, license holders were required to operate in the "public interest, convenience and necessity." What those words actually mean is a matter of interpretation.

In order to make sure that broadcasting was locally based,

ownership was originally limited to five AM stations, five FM stations, and seven television stations. Only five of the television stations could be on the preferred VHF (2–13) channels. Ownership limits have been changed many times over the years and are a continuing source of disagreement between owners and public interest groups.

Unlike the printed—and later, digital—press, radio and television stations were not given the full benefit of the First Amendment. Their use of government-owned frequencies meant stations also held a measure of accountability to both Congress and the FCC. What exactly does this mean? No one actually knows. Broadcasters contend they have full First Amendment press rights. Others disagree. Congress and federal agency policies vary from party to party and even administration to administration.

What no one disputes is the government's right to impose noncontent regulations, such as rules for children's programming, closed captioning, descriptive captioning, and other areas. To put this another way, the government cannot tell a licensee what to say, but it can demand that whatever is said should be available to all users.

Neither are the rules simple or clear-cut. An expletive at 7:00 p.m. can cause a station to be fined, but that same expletive at 11:00 p.m. might be perfectly OK.

Moreover, television stations are regulated by multiple government agencies. The FCC is the primary regulator, but the FTC ensures broadcasters treat all commercial clients fairly. The Federal Aviation Administration regulates some aspects of television station towers. The list goes on.

Dealing with regulation is a critical part of any general manager's responsibility. That means being up-to-date on all regulations. Every company retains private counsel who are experts in broadcast regulation. Most of those companies, as well as the National Association of Broadcasters (NAB), regularly update clients. Whatever method your company chooses, make sure you are fully engaged.

Fines for running afoul of government regulations are bad enough, but neither do you want to be the source of embarrassment to your company among its peers. In some extreme cases, stations have lost their licenses to operate.

Lobbying

As important a role as federal agencies play in television, the role of Congress is even more important. From the advent of broadcasting Congress has been passing regulations designed to meet the political ends of its members.

During the early 1970s, to aid the launch of cable television, Congress allowed cable systems to carry local television stations without permission of or payment to the stations. The 1992 Cable Act ended this loophole and resulted in today's retransmission consent system.

During the 1970s, Congress limited the number of hours a network could produce in prime time in the hope of adding diverse local programming to communities. They got *Wheel of Fortune* instead. During that era, Congress also limited network ownership of programming, a ban that was lifted forty years later.

Congressional relaxation of radio station ownership and later television station ownership resulted, with a few notable exceptions, in the end of local ownership.

Whatever you think of what Congress has done in the past, one thing is for sure. It will continue to pass laws in the future that will have unexpected consequences.

An important player in the passing of future legislation is the local general manager, many of whom have strong relationships with local members of Congress. As one of those general managers, you are the linchpin of success or failure of broadcaster-related legislation. Why? Because you speak directly to every member's constituents.

The NAB, in coordination with state associations, does a great job of identifying issues and helping set priorities, but it would be powerless without the local relationships general managers build with members of the House and Senate.

I can tell you from experience that virtually every member of your congressional delegation will welcome a relationship with you. They are constantly running for office. You are in charge of the most important bullhorn in their district. Both parties gain from the relationship.

Building Relationships

Building a relationship means exactly that. Relationships don't start with an ask. The best time to begin building a relationship is when there are no broadcast issues in front of Congress. The more you meet with a member, the more likely it is you will get to a first-name basis.

Talk about what the member wants to talk about, but at some point, you need to also talk about the critical services you supply to the community: emergency alerts, severe weather, breaking news. Laying this groundwork is critical because at some point down the line, you will be asking for support. Let's say you need the member's support on not changing retransmission consent rules. It's easy to explain why retransmission payments are critical to the station's emergency / news / public service role if the member already understands what that role is.

In-Station Meetings

It is important that every time a member of Congress or a key state or local politician is in the station, you are notified. Ideally, the politician is brought to your office before going to the interview. This gives you a chance to say hello on your turf. It is also a reminder that you head an important media organization. Always thank the politician for coming by.

The in-station meeting is also an opportunity to invite the politician to lunch. If the answer is yes—and it is always yes, though sometimes with a vague "down the road"—you can then call the local office and ask them to set a date.

Never use lunch to lobby. This is an opportunity to enhance a first-name relationship. If you spend it asking for something, it will likely be your last lunch. Talking about industry issues that affect the member's constituents is fine. Just don't turn a conversation into pressure.

Multistation Meetings

Many state associations set up occasional market-wide GM meetings with a member of Congress, either in the member's office or at a private lunch. Unlike individual lunches, this is your opportunity to talk about and lobby for important issues. Normally, a talking point agenda is prepared and sent to all GMs before the meeting. The best associations also decide beforehand which GM will take the lead on which issue. Because the state associations represent both television and radio, there will always be some radio-only issues to discuss.

DC Meetings

The NAB sponsors an annual gathering of state associations in Washington, DC, to discuss key issues, followed by a day of in-person lobbying on the Hill. The fly-in is one of the most important functions of the NAB / state association partnership because it allows broadcasters to present a joint nationwide voice on industry issues.

Like all other association functions, both television and radio are included.

State Lobbying

While not as critical as federal regulations, state laws also have a profound effect on broadcasters. To ignore state lobbying is to find yourself with unpleasant surprises, such as tower regulations or the elimination of contract noncompetes.

State associations also take the lead on in-state issues, but remember, the real power is with you, the head of a local television station.

Your Responsibility

Lobbying is important. Broadcasters are often arrayed against heavily financed organizations representing a wide range of industries seeking legislation not in our best interest. Many of these organizations make significant campaign contributions, far greater than broadcasters are in a position to match.

To be a great general manager, you must also become a great lobbyist. That means being on a first-name basis with both of your senators and every member of Congress whose district you serve so that you will be able to make a clear, compelling case for legislation you believe to be in both the public's interest and the station's interest.

Summary

The United States is unique in the world because from the beginning, broadcasting was based on the idea of private ownership of stations at a time when most other governments elected to create national semigovernmental organizations.

In return for licenses to operate on the public airways, television stations agree to act in the "public interest, convenience and necessity." Exactly what that phrase means continues to evolve and be the subject of debate.

Because of the wide range of government bureaus that regulate television, in addition to the FCC, general managers must maintain up-to-date knowledge on every important issue. To not do so invites fines and industry embarrassment. In some extreme cases, stations have lost their licenses to operate.

Because Congress is the ultimate decider of communications policy, lobbying is a critical part of every general manager's responsibility. This means building personal relationships with every member of Congress in a station's viewing area.

Legislators on all levels, not just federal, welcome relationships with local station general managers because those stations serve the same constituencies as do the politicians.

Key Takeaways

- Television stations operate on publicly owned airways. For this reason, they are required to operate in the "public interest, convenience and necessity."
- A wide number of federal agencies regulate television stations. General managers must always be up-to-date.
- Congress is the ultimate regulator of television.
- Because members of Congress share the same constituencies as television stations, politicians welcome relationships with local general managers.
- Great general managers are also great lobbyists.

22

MANAGING UP

Over the years, I've had all kinds of bosses. A few were truly great leaders whom I respected and was glad to work for. Others were so different from me that I've had to adjust my own style to make the relationship work. One or two were just plain terrible, creating unneeded stress for everyone they came into contact with, including me. What all those group heads share is that, like you and me, they are fallible human beings trying to do a good job.

We have no control over who our boss will be, but we do control our side of the relationship. Like every other aspect of being a general manager, it is important to think this through, trying to understand things from your boss's perspective.

By the time you become a general manager, you have experienced the sobering fact that the higher you get in an organization, the less direct control you have over daily operations, the fewer confidants you can trust, and the more isolated you become. We've discussed these things in other chapters. They are genuine obstacles you must understand and then work hard to overcome.

With your own situation in mind, think how isolated your group head must be. He or she has almost no direct control over station operations, has even fewer confidants than you do, and is in some ways completely isolated. At least you can walk around the station and talk to people. Your boss can't even do that. And don't forget your boss has a boss, which also complicates the relationship.

Almost every person I've known who has moved from general manager to corporate executive has told me how much they miss the hustle and bustle of working in a television station. When I first went to work for Frank Magid, I was assigned to the Chicago office, a quiet office building where I had very little contact with other consultants. I hated every minute in that building. There was no energy, no urgency, nothing to spur the creative process. The eventual move to Cedar Rapids, Iowa, where I was in daily contact with other consultants, was a relief, but even that atmosphere had a certain sense of formality foreign to the station experience.

In addition to those factors, your boss has the pressure of working in a political atmosphere that adds additional complications. Understanding the pressures on your boss is important because it helps you craft a relationship that benefits you both.

Communication

Here's a shock. General managers sometimes withhold information from their group head. Other times, they shade the facts to make themselves look better. It's not right, but it happens. I'm sure every group head has experienced some measure of this. Department heads sometimes do the same thing to you, but at least you are in the station where you have multiple sources of information. If a department head is being less than straightforward, you find out pretty quickly.

One of the most important things you can do for your boss is to make sure you always provide the truth, even when it makes you look bad.

A good start is to make sure you are providing as much information as possible. You have to be careful because you do not want to invite input on daily decision-making. Daily decision-making is your province, but you still must make sure your boss knows the important things going on in the station. Most of these things you will report in the past tense, but this also gives you an opportunity to look forward, laying the groundwork for those decisions your boss will want to be involved with.

For instance, hiring employees like account executives, photographers, and producers are not decisions your boss would normally be involved with. Hiring department heads or major talent is another story. Not only do you want to lay the groundwork for these kinds of hires, you want your boss's input as a second opinion. I can't imagine buying an important syndicated program without input from both my boss and the corporate programming person. Nor can I imagine firing someone without giving my boss warning. Be smart about it. Your boss probably has more experience than you do, so there are times his or her input can be helpful.

By keeping your boss informed, you build credibility. General managers without credibility find themselves constantly second-guessed, and that is the last thing you want.

Hopefully, your group head is someone who will appreciate the way you communicate, but what happens when your styles come into conflict?

When Styles Conflict

My first GM job was working for a guy who wanted me to call him every day with a list of station issues. I did my best for eighteen months, then I could not deal with it anymore. Having him so intimately involved with everyday decisions was driving me crazy. I wanted to do things his way, but I simply could not. We

235

finally had a meeting in which I told him I couldn't continue to operate that way. People in the station had seen what was going on and considered me to be just a puppet without real authority to run the station. Telling my boss I could not continue operating the way he wanted were hard words to get out of my mouth. I expected to get fired or at least to be put in my place, but instead, he just looked at me. So I went back to the station and started making daily decisions without talking to him about everything that came up.

Having staked out a position with my boss, I was in unchartered territory, so I tried to give him as much information as I could, for the most part doing it after the fact. I stopped calling every day and reduced my calls to one day a week. I got no feedback until three years later when one of the company's large market stations got in trouble. Out of the blue, I was asked to go run it. It was a stunning call. I expected to be the last person he would promote.

Even after I was in place at the new station, we still disagreed on how much he should be involved with daily decisions. I can only conclude that the relationship worked because he knew I would always tell him the truth. Our styles were completely different, but we had come to respect each other. It was an odd situation, but it worked.

Although I eventually ran the company's most profitable station, taking a position with my boss that was opposed to his natural style pretty much ensured I would never be given a corporate role, which was OK. I was a station guy to the core.

Three Important Rules

If there is one rule when giving information to your boss, it is this: always tell the truth. Never twist the facts to make them look better. Never avoid difficult situations. Never conceal the truth. We are all tempted to do these things from time to time for a host of reasons, but being less than straightforward is a trap that will eventually ensnare you. You run the risk of destroying your credibility with the single most important person in your professional life.

The second rule is to make sure bad news travels fast and goes all the way up the chain. If you can't reach your boss, call the next person up the line. It is easy to rationalize not giving your boss bad news quickly. Maybe we don't have all the facts yet. Maybe things will get better. None of those is a good argument for not calling your boss to say, "I have bad news. We don't know all the facts yet, but . . ."

Third, never blindside your boss. If something bad is going on, make sure your boss gets that information from you, not someone else. The same pressures that cause a general manager to shade the truth or avoid a difficult situation come into play here. The worst thing you can do to your boss is have him or her learn something important about your station from someone other than you. Even worse, you don't want your boss to hear it from his or her boss!

Building a Positive Relationship

Positive relationships begin with your competence and ability to do your job, so let's assume you understand your job, are not in over your head, and are successful at running your station. Given that baseline, how do you become someone seen as one of the great general managers in your company? Here are some keys to building that level of respect.

Let's begin with how you communicate. Because we are human, our first instinct is to always show how smart, competent, and great we are. We also instinctively avoid blame, even when something is clearly our fault. If we succumb to those temptations, we will eventually learn that always trying to make ourselves look good usually has the opposite effect. Praising yourself is never well received. Far better to cultivate a reputation for transparency and straight talk.

Admitting when you make a mistake builds credibility, providing you are not making the same mistakes over and over. It also builds credibility to take responsibility for a bad decision a department head made but you might have prevented. General managers known for always throwing their subordinates under the bus look petty and small. This damages credibility. The best general managers support their department heads while still being honest about their capabilities.

Two great things happen when you establish a reputation for straight talk and transparency. First, your boss sees you as someone who will always tell the truth. Second, you stand out from general managers who are less transparent. Both those things set you apart.

Let's assume your group head oversees twelve general managers. The group head probably doesn't have a physical list ranking general managers, but they are ranked nonetheless. You want to be at the top of that ranking. General managers in the top echelon spend far less time dealing with their boss as well as other corporate people. They are asked to explain their decisions far less. In short, they are left alone to do their jobs without someone second-guessing every decision.

Bottom Line Matters

So far, we have not discussed how bottom-line performance affects your relationship with your boss. Consistently positive and better-than-planned bottom-line performance can overcome a wealth of other shortcomings. I've known several general managers who were not highly regarded in their companies but always seemed to drive bottom-line success. That success kept them in their jobs.

Consistent bottom-line success is rare in any station. Sometimes ratings, revenue, and profits are up; other times, they are down. There are a great number of factors out of our control that help or hurt our station's performance. Plus, there are no perfect general managers. We all make mistakes. Every general manager is going to experience a time of rocky performance.

What happens when your station is at one of those low points? Does the group head start to second-guess your work? Do you suddenly find everything the station does being scrutinized? Do you begin to worry about your job? If you have built the right relationship with your boss, none of those things happens because she or he trusts your ability to do the job. If you need help, you will either get support or judgment. There is no question which one you want.

When to Stand Up to Your Boss

You cannot control what your group head does, but that does not mean you can't play an important part in setting the boundaries of the relationship.

I once knew a group head that was infamous for going into stations and finding something he thought should be changed. In one case, during his first meeting with the general manager, the group head told her that her newsroom was a bad background for the news set and that she should build a wall between the two. Her response was that his idea was interesting and she would think about it, but the current background worked very well.

What the general manager did was set a reasonable boundary for the group head's input. She was respectful and did not dismiss the idea outright, but neither did she rush out and immediately change the station's news set. She also grew the relationship by agreeing with some of his thoughts and implementing his ideas when they made sense to her.

Contrast this with another general manager who was known for doing everything the group head suggested without question. In effect, the group head was running the station. That hurt morale, lowered staff opinion of the general manager's leadership, and created stress throughout the building.

In both of these situations, the group head and general managers were talking about suggestions and recommendations, not direct orders. If a group head says you have to do something, then do it. If you disagree, then make that known, but don't whine or complain. You have been overruled, so move on.

Let me be absolutely clear. When a general manager does not stand up to a group head, that is the general manager's fault, not the group head's.

The two examples I just shared really happened. Guess which general manager the group head probably had the most respect for?

Bad Group Heads

In three decades of running stations, I've seen some bad group heads. Thankfully, most were people I didn't work for. I've seen general managers stressed out so much they hated going to work. A few experienced health problems. One exploded, quit his job, and walked out.

If you find yourself in an intolerable situation, don't go it alone. Find someone who can give you solid, confidential advice that will put the situation in perspective.

If all else fails, find another job. Life is too short.

That does not mean you should quit without a job. Wait until you have the right thing lined up. You don't want to go from one bad situation to another, so take your time. Knowing you are going to eventually leave can take a lot of pressure off.

Before leaving, make sure you have done everything on your part to make your current situation work. Also, ask yourself what you have learned that will help make your next relationship successful.

Two-Way Relationships

You cannot operate effectively without the support of your group head, but support is a two-way street. A boss that believes in what you are doing is invaluable to success. One that does not fully trust you becomes a stumbling block. Which one you get is usually up to you.

Summary

Keep your boss in perspective. Bosses come in all shapes and sizes. Like you, they are fallible human beings trying to do their job. You have no control over who your boss is, but you do control your side of the relationship.

There are many reasons why a general manager might withhold important information from his or her boss, but none of those reasons is a good one. Sharing honest information is an important way to build trust and credibility.

Remember three important rules: Always tell the truth. Make sure bad news travels fast. Never blindside your boss. Breaking any of these rules can damage your relationship.

Building a relationship with your boss is important to your current well-being and your future career. Your boss is dealing with a wide range of general managers and competencies. Make sure you are at the top of the trusted list.

There are times when you must stand up to your boss. Respectfully disagreeing builds respect. Being a puppet destroys respect.

If you are working for a truly terrible boss, don't go it alone. Get professional help. If you then decide to leave, do it the right way.

The kind of relationship you have with your boss is usually up to you.

Key Takeaways

- Like you, your boss is a fallible human being.
- Always tell the truth.
- Make sure bad news travels fast.
- Never blindside your boss.
- When appropriate, be willing to respectfully disagree.
- The kind of relationship you have with your boss is up to you.

23

THE FUTURE

As I said in the preface, it's hard to believe that two decades into the twenty-first century, local television is still a viable business, much less our single most important form of communication. Because we live in a world of fragmented media and constant change, it is easy to forget that local television is not just viable; it is the last form of mass communication. Only local television is able to collectively bring tens of millions of viewers to a single screen at the same time.

Yes, television newscasts do tend to look alike, and core news viewers are getting older. A changing landscape of choice, connectivity, and portability means younger consumers live in a broader world than their parents, causing them to see television news as an option, not a requirement. They often prefer for media to be on demand, not appointment based. They also define news differently from their elders. None of this means younger viewers don't value television. It means television, especially television news, must adapt to the viewer, not the other way around.

The purpose of this book is not to be an apologist for television as we have known it. It is to empower those who lead local stations to not just adapt to the future but to create it. This is not a defensive play. It is about using existing massive launchpads to create something more exciting and even more profitable in the future than what we have today.

The timing for creating that future could not be better. The marginalization of local newspapers, the historically low levels of trust in national media, and the Wild West of internet information have created an opportunity for leading television stations to use the power of their trusted brands to create a new and dynamic relationship with local news consumers—one that transcends platforms. It is not about a platform. It is about becoming the consumer's most trusted source of information.

Local television stations are unique in that they answer directly to the constituents they serve. In the old days, viewers were quick to call or write a letter with a complaint. Some still do, especially if their favorite program is interrupted, and stations still get a fair number of e-mails, but the pervasiveness of social media is now our most instant feedback. Not all feedback is credible, but all of it is worth hearing. If a great number people are complaining about the same thing, you likely have a problem. If a significant group of people like something, that information can also be valuable.

Direct responsibility to our user base is what distinguishes our businesses from those based in New York, Los Angeles, or Silicon Valley. It is easy for someone at a network to dismiss a message from a viewer in Des Moines. Not so for the general manager of that network's Des Moines affiliate.

Because digital platforms are all measurable, stations now have not only direct feedback but an accurate measurement of user behavior. Those are good things. Journalistically, they mean a station's news product can be more responsive than ever before. From an advertising point of view, stations can provide targeted access to specific end users.

Make no mistake, journalism is not dying. Every study of young consumers shows two things. First, each new generation defines news differently from their parents and grandparents. Second, they have an incredible interest in news. Because our television platforms have been so financially successful, it has been easy to ignore changes in the consumer. Now is the time for us to become willing to think in terms of consumers' interests, needs, content preferences, and delivery systems.

Those two facts about consumers, and our willingness to act on them, are the reasons television-based local news brands have reason to be optimistic. The enemy to positive action and growth is culture, which is why culture plays such a prominent role in this book.

Narrow culture-driven thinking causes us to waste time worrying about the future of our linear television platforms when we should be thinking about the launchpads those platforms represent today—both for traditional television delivery and a host of exploding new opportunities. The future is not about old-versus-new media; it is about appropriate media for the task.

None of this means linear television is going away. ATSC 3.0 and 5G interactivity are just the beginning of an exciting, integrated future. Quality and picture size will continue to grow. New technology will add an unimaginable opportunity for in and out of home screens.

As media becomes more personalized, consumers will demand more and more from their most trusted sources of local news—not news slanted to their views but information they can bank on as being true. Sure, some people watch Fox News or MSNBC because of their perceived perspectives, but that is not the future. Good, bad, or indifferent, people want the truth and they want it from someone they trust.

Trust is the key issue. The older generation of viewers who only knew newspapers and television were institutionally oriented. They trusted institutions. That began to change in the late 1960s, but it was only when people began to share information through personal handheld devices that the much more powerful dynamic of cohort trust came into play.

Understanding the difference between institutional trust and cohort trust is foundational for television stations that want to morph from "television news" to "trusted local news brand that includes television news." When newspapers and television stations dominated the media conversation, their gatekeeper role was naturally top down. Both institutions and consumers understood the rules. When the twin tsunamis of choice and connectivity moved power to the end user, consumers quickly gained control of the conversation. Unfortunately, most newspapers and television stations chose to not notice. That meant the end of many newspapers. It does not have to mean the end of television.

Even today, stations are reluctant to acknowledge the new reality of consumers setting the agenda. Because stations still have large and viable audiences, over-the-air local television advertising is still highly valuable, not to mention the addition of valuable retransmission fees. That current profitability makes it harder to see the incredible opportunities just over the horizon.

Nowhere is the opportunity greater than in local news and local information. Not every station will benefit from the future, but for some, there will be greater opportunities than anything we had in the past.

Of course, the future is not just news. Programming fees to networks, funded by retransmission revenue, mean traditional over-the-air networks now have the resources to continue being viable. That allows big events, such as the Super Bowl, to continue to bring viewers and attention to local affiliates. Why are multiple-system-operators (MSOs) willing to pay retransmission fees? Because of consumer demand for local news and big events that are available no other way.

As MSOs lose viewers to cord cutting and over-the-top (OTT) providers, we should note that traditional over-the-air television is a primary component of every new stream, be it delivered via box or directly to an OTT device. Anybody who watches television sports using an antenna will tell you the over-the-air signal of local television stations is superior to the highly compressed versions delivered by cable.

The march forward to new technology always continues, so it is important we put the role of technology in perspective as it pertains to the future of local television. Technology is a double-edged sword. It creates new opportunities for consumers, but it also creates opportunities for content providers. Without content, technology is meaningless.

Consumers only have twenty-four hours in a day, so any new activity that uses time cuts into previous activities. But the real issue is not technology. The issue is how consumers choose to use their time. That is why brand, which is the determiner of how a consumer spends her time and money, is so important.

In an earlier chapter I quoted John Lavine's three reasons why consumers use brand to make decisions. They are worth repeating here.

Ever-Rising Content

During the next hour, more information will be created than during any other hour in the history of the world. No one can keep up with the overwhelming choices they face each day.

Increasing Complexity

The world is constantly becoming more difficult to navigate. Every new operating system, from cars to phones to home appliances, now has a learning curve. Formerly simple acts now require complicated decisions.

Lack of Time

Every person is limited to 1,440 minutes per day. If that person sleeps 8 hours, she has 960 minutes left. Some studies show working women have less than 17 minutes per day to do whatever they want.

Brand

In order to navigate today's complex and demanding world, consumers automatically create shortcuts we call brands. Brands allow the consumer to instantly recognize things important to his or her life. It also allows the consumer to automatically reject things not perceived as important. Both are done without conscious thought.

Once a brand is established in the consumer's mind, it is incredibly difficult to change. In most circumstances, brand can only be changed by long-term repetition of unique consumer value. There is, however, another way to change brand: during major events that so affect a person's life, his or her perception of a particular brand or brands can be changed. This is most commonly seen in television during natural or man-made traumatic events when one television station provides the best coverage by far.

The most important thing to understand about brand is that it is rooted in reality, not advertising or wishful thinking. In order for brand to change, reality must change.

Overcoming Twentieth-Century Roots

The early 1980s, when I was a consultant with Frank N. Magid Associates, were heady times for young consultants. We were able to travel the country, give advice, and be paid for it. Consulting could be an ego-building experience because stations assumed we were uniquely equipped to help them win the ratings war. Everywhere we went, people hung on our every word.

It is interesting to look back and realize that we were not actually inventing anything at all. We were simply taking good ideas from one station and injecting them into others. Everything from a desk with two anchors; to a weatherperson on one side and sports on the other; to the way we did live shots, reporter packages, graphics, and other elements were all things we saw in one market and then introduced to another. As a result, all news came to look and feel pretty much the same. We were homogenizing news. That homogenization continues even now.

It was not a problem in those days for all television news to look and feel the same. Television viewership was exploding, as was news viewing. There were plenty of viewers to go around.

Imagine, for a moment, back to 1980. The average American home had two television sets, a radio, and a stereo record player. It subscribed to a morning newspaper, which might be read at night. That was it for in-home entertainment. No cable, no internet, no wireless devices of any kind. VCRs were a rarity. Even CDs did not exist. The only books were printed on paper.

Not only were in-home options limited, the average community only had four television stations: CBS, NBC, ABC, and PBS.

This environment of limited choice meant households overwhelmingly watched network television. There was simply nothing else to watch. Stations and networks competed with each other because there were no other competitors. Television programmers even talked about something they called the theory of the least objectionable program. According to this theory, virtually everyone watched television at night. If there was not a program on they wanted to see, they would choose the least objectionable. Choices were limited to the four channels available.

When choices are limited, power moves to whoever controls the choices. In this case, power moved both to networks and local stations. That meant stations only had to compete against each other for viewer attention. With plenty of viewers to go around, even last-place news stations did well financially.

Today, user choices are virtually unlimited, meaning power has moved to the chooser. In fact, today's consumer has a myriad of other choices besides the home television because it's just about impossible to find a media-free space in today's world. You can't pump gas without being forced to view a screen. You can't sit on a plane and just read a book—each seat has a screen 10 inches in front of your face and if you don't want to watch your screen, good luck ignoring your seatmates' screens.

None of these things existed back during the 1980's. As you read this, choices continue to explode, but one thing remains constant: each consumer still has only twenty-four hours a day to perform all activities, including sleep.

In the 1980s, consumers almost universally watched television news. There were simply no other choices. Today's consumers do not have to watch television news, so they only do so when they choose. Unfortunately for us, some choose to never watch at all.

Moving from Old Viewers to Young Loyalists

Who are today's loyal television news viewers? Look at any rating book and you will see they are overwhelmingly over fifty years of age. The older they are, the more loyal to television news they are. Of course, we still have a significant number of younger viewers. We even continue to add some very young viewers, but the statistics are clear. Linear news audiences are continuing to age with fewer younger viewers being added than ever before.

For many years, it was an article of faith in television news that when viewers turned thirty, with families and responsibilities, they would begin to watch television news even though it had not been of interest to them in the past. That is no longer true. There is reason to believe it may never have been true. We were simply kidding ourselves. When young people begin to raise families, they do become more interested in their communities, but that does not necessarily mean they start watching television news.

None of this is new or surprising, which makes our response to viewer erosion fascinating. For the first twenty years or so, we ignored it. During the 2008 recession, we panicked. Today, thanks to local television's current position as the last form of mass media, plus an injection of retransmission revenue, we are back to ignoring it.

One thing we are doing right is attempting to extend our brands to new platforms—not only mobile and web but over-the-top and other emerging technologies. The practices we hold dear when it comes to producing television news are also being extended to those platforms. What we have not been doing is tailoring our presentations to take advantage of the unique benefits each new platform offers.

Though the world, viewers, and technology have all grown, we have not changed our basic assumptions about what television news is and how it should be presented. Therein, at least in my view, lies the opportunity—providing we are willing to look at our business the same way viewers do.

Younger people do not dislike television. In fact, they love it. They love it so much they are willing to pay cable companies, over-the-top providers, Netflix, and a world of other sources hard cash every month to watch the programs they care about. Because traditional television news still enjoys credibility, during breaking news or a crisis, the first place those younger viewers turn to continues to be their local stations. The problem is that on a day-to-day basis, they do not feel compelled to watch local television news in its current form.

People have both a want and need for local news, but they are choosing to not watch it. Why? Could it be that the way we produce and present news is no longer relevant to their lives? Could the problem also be our definition of news?

It does not have to be this way. If we are willing to take a fresh look at television as local news providers, we can create a product for the future that will be viable and highly profitable. The way to begin is to take our heads out of the sand, look at the world around us with fresh eyes, and change our culture to become user oriented instead of producer oriented.

As I've tried to make clear other places in this book, radical change that makes viewers uncomfortable is not the answer. Change must be carefully made over an extended period of time; that way, radical change does not look like radical change.

Of course, those of us who have spent our lives in television news must first overcome our own cultural biases that prevent us from seeing a clear picture. One way to start is to look at a related industry's experience.

Newspaper Failure Is a Key Lesson

We have already discussed in detail the lessons television can learn from newspapers, so I won't repeat them here. Newspapers had the strongest brands in media, but their inability to overcome their own cultures prevented them from morphing into something not just new but far more valuable.

The Trusted Source

No one wants to get up every morning, go through every possible news story, and then decide what is true and what is not. Everyone wants a trusted source. That trusted source may be your best friend, but it can also be a news organization.

The quest for truth is an inborn characteristic of human beings. Even news consumers who are loyal viewers of a particular cable network understand when that network is taking a political position. That does not mean consumers limit intake of news and information to one brand.

Not only can a local television–based brand be a trusted source, it has the added advantage of covering local news and information, meaning it does not have to compete with national media.

News consumers will accept information they do not want to hear if it is coming from a source they trust. Why? Because the source never lies, never slants, never tries to impose an agenda. If a television-based brand becomes a consumer's trusted source, everything else follows.

Being a trusted source also means understanding the consumer. How does the consumer define news? What does the consumer care about? Why does the consumer think a particular thing matters? That does not mean pandering to the consumer. It means understanding a world that is far broader than a seven-minute A block in a television newscast.

Consumers Control the Future

Though we've talked about consumers in terms of media consumption, it is worth noting that consumers are now in control of far more than just media. Today's consumers are wealthier in terms of disposable income than ever before. Thanks to years of paying cell phone and cable bills, today's consumers are also used to paying dollars for what they want. The launch of Netflix would be unthinkable back during the 1980's because consumers were not yet conditioned to paying for niche media.

The same consumer trends we see in media are reflected in virtually every other industry from consumer goods to service industries. The consumer is king.

Television Uniquely Positioned

Looking forward, no other form of media, no other technology, no other local organization rivals the current position that leading television stations enjoy in their communities. Local stations are the natural launchpads to future media brands that dominate local news and information. As the general manager of a leading station, making that happen is up to you.

Summary

In spite of an aging news audience, local television is not only still a viable business; it continues to be the single most important means of communication. No other service can claim the same relationship local television stations enjoy with the communities they serve.

Because consumers live in a broader world than ours, building the future means understanding that world and filling its needs. Younger consumers love television but, unlike older viewers, see it as one news option, not an appointment that must be kept every day. That does not take away from television's value.

Our timing for creating the future could not be better. Television stations have a unique bond with viewers unlike that which any national service is able to provide. Because stations are directly responsible to their consumers, they cannot ignore changes in those consumers.

Consumers use brands to make decisions because it is a shortcut that saves time in a world of overwhelming information, ever-increasing complexity, and inelastic time.

Culture is one of the most powerful forces in life. Understanding how our current culture was created gives us perspective on how to create the future.

Every consumer wants a trusted source. Becoming that source is a complex proposition because it means understanding the consumer, seeing the consumer's perspective, then filling those needs without pandering. Telling consumers some things they do not want to hear is a critical part of building the kind of brand that will become a trusted source.

Finally

With the continuing explosion of both video platforms and video content, it would be easy to think of local television as a technology from the past, a linear service locked into local news and network programming at fixed times every day. That would be wrong because today's local television is about far more than the mechanics of technology; it is about a relationship.

Local television is a direct path to the future of local news and information. Technologies will come and go, as will competitors and threats, but great local news and information brands will become even more powerful because they will be built on a simple pact with the consumers they serve.

Brands will provide trustworthy local news, information, and data. Some of that news will look like the content we provide today, but other products will be far different, tailored to individual wants and needs. In return, local consumers will contribute not only time and cash but actual content. The result will be an incredibly rich, constantly evolving experience.

I'm a second-generation broadcaster who was fortunate to know some of the people who invented local television. Experiencing the decades between then and now has been an incredible experience, but if I could start again today, I would. The future will be something to behold.

Key Takeaways

- Local television is the last form of mass media.
- Because their lives are complex, consumers make decisions based on brand.
- Consumers live in a broader world than ours. Understanding that world is the key to brand building.
- The most important local news brand is the trusted source.
- The unique bond television stations enjoy with viewers makes television the natural leader to the future.
- The future is going to be more exciting and more rewarding than anything we can imagine today.
- As the general manager of a leading station, building the future is your responsibility.

ACKNOWLEDGMENTS

Going from rough manuscript to published book is a group effort. Thanks to my publisher, Lily Coyle, whose ever-present wit and eye for detail made the project fun; superb editors Sara and Chris Ensey, who made it a better book; proofreader Paige Polinsky, whose final polish is evident; Laura Drew, whose bold design makes the book stand out, and Becca Hart, outstanding project coordinator. Thanks also to Susan Adams Lloyd, a leader in her own right, who first suggested I work with Lily.

I'd also like to thank the following general managers and group heads: M. D. Smith IV, who taught me the joy of winning; the late Bob Regalbuto, who proved leadership is also theater; the late Billy Brooks, who taught me leadership begins with caring about people; Jim Ellis, who helped guide me back to stations; Dow Smith, who taught me to think big and bigger; Ron Townsend, who modeled leadership every day; Ed Pfeiffer, who taught me negotiation and may have invented showmanship; Cecil Walker, who made me a general manager twice and proved different-thinking people could do great things together; Mel Karmazin, whose sheer determination sometimes trumped everything else; Mark DeSantis, who proved leadership was more important than ownership; Stu Kellogg, whose leadership models his faith; Emily Barr, who is the same person as a CEO as she was as an intern; Tony Vinciquerra, who rescued me from CBS; David Barrett, who made Hearst Television the nation's best television company; Jordan Wertlieb, who is leading Hearst Television into an even-greater future; and to my dear friend, and great Hearst leader, Mike Hayes.

Thanks to John Lavine, mentor and brilliant thinker; Dr. Deborah Wenger, who gave me the opportunity to write a book with her; and Dean Will Norton, who sometimes allows me to misguide students at Ole Miss.

To inspired leaders Glenn Haygood, Dan Joerres, Jim Berman, Michelle Butt, Jeff Bartlett, John Remes, Janet Mason, and a dozen others whose names I will remember as soon as the book goes to press. To each of those not listed, my apologies.

To my son Pepper (who goes by Hank), my son Norman (who goes by Harper), and my beautiful daughter-in-law, Courtney. Finally, to the love of my life and partner, Maria, who raised the kids, bought and sold the houses, and still puts up with me.

INDEX